THE PSYCHOLOGY OF SCHOOL BULLYING

Why do children get involved with bullying? Does cyberbullying differ from traditional bullying? How can bullying at school be prevented?

The Psychology of School Bullying explores what bullying is and what factors lead to children playing roles as bullies, victims, defenders, bystanders or even some combination of these. The book examines proactive strategies to reduce the likelihood of bullying happening in school, but also looks at what action the school could take if bullying incidents do occur.

As bullying can have such far-reaching consequences and sometimes tragic outcomes, it is vital to grasp how and why it happens, and *The Psychology of School Bullying* shows how improved knowledge and understanding can lead to effective interventions.

Peter K. Smith is Emeritus Professor of Psychology at Goldsmiths, University of London, UK. He has written and edited many books and articles on the topic of school bullying. In 2015 he was awarded the William Thierry Preyer award for Excellence in Research on Human Development.

THE PSYCHOLOGY OF EVERYTHING

The *Psychology of Everything* is a series of books which debunk the myths and pseudo-science surrounding some of life's biggest questions.

The series explores the hidden psychological factors that drive us, from our sub-conscious desires and aversions, to the innate social instincts handed to us across the generations. Accessible, informative, and always intriguing, each book is written by an expert in the field, examining how research-based knowledge compares with popular wisdom, and illustrating the potential of psychology to enrich our understanding of humanity and modern life.

Applying a psychological lens to an array of topics and contemporary concerns – from sex to addiction to conspiracy theories – The *Psychology of Everything* will make you look at everything in a new way.

Titles in the series:

For further information about this series please visit www.thepsychologyofeverything.co.uk.

THE PSYCHOLOGY OF SCHOOL BULLYING

PETER K. SMITH

Routledge
Taylor & Francis Group

LONDON AND NEW YORK

First published 2019
by Routledge
2 Park Square, Milton Park, Abingdon, Oxon OX14 4RN

and by Routledge
711 Third Avenue, New York, NY 10017

Routledge is an imprint of the Taylor & Francis Group, an informa business

British Library Cataloguing-in-Publication Data
A catalogue record for this book is available from the British Library

Library of Congress Cataloging-in-Publication Data
A catalog record for this book has been requested

ISBN: 978-1-138-69939-7 (hbk)
ISBN: 978-1-138-69940-3 (pbk)
ISBN: 978-1-315-51689-9 (ebk)

Typeset in Joanna
by Apex CoVantage, LLC

Visit https://www.routledge.com/The-Psychology-of-Everything/
book-series/POE
Printed and bound by CPI Group (UK) Ltd, Croydon, CR0 4YY

CONTENTS

1

WHAT IS BULLYING IN SCHOOL AND HOW HAS IT BEEN STUDIED?

Bullying is an evocative term. Most people will have witnessed it or experienced it in one form or another. But only since the 1980s has there been serious interest, both from researchers and from the wider community. Much of this was sparked by tragic events such as suicides due to being bullied at school, publicized by the media. This chapter will outline what we mean by bullying, the history behind the study of it, and the main forms it takes, including the development of cyberbullying this century. The book as a whole is about bullying at school, or among school-aged pupils. But of course bullying can happen at college, at home, in the workplace and in other institutions. Some brief mention of these will be made in the final chapter. But for many people, bullying conjures up images of childhood, and of suffering which can be difficult to redress.

Let's start with a couple of examples. The first is from a book by Rosemary Hayes and Carrie Herbert, called *Rising above bullying* and published in 2011.[1] It contains a number of case studies of severely bullied children. One is of Zac (not his real name), aged 17 at the time of writing. He describes how:

> It started when I went to middle school, the taunting and name-calling . . . At first it was only a couple of boys but soon

it became a class game . . . it began to spread through the school . . . Some of the class above started calling me names and even some of the younger kids. The taunts followed me round wherever I went . . . "No one likes you. Why don't you go and put your head in the toilet?" . . . it was at secondary school that it got really bad. At home I began to have nightmares about what they'd do to me the next day . . . They'd be waiting for me. . . . I could never relax. . . . The nightmares didn't stop.

Zac eventually stopped going to school but later got into a Red Balloon Learner Centre (see Chapter 6). He writes that "Slowly I regained some confidence and some enjoyment of life . . . I have flashbacks . . . though these are getting fewer . . . that happy, confident boy has gone for ever – but at least I have a future now".

The second example comes from a book by Diana and Victoria Webster, called *So many Everests*, published in 2010.[2] Victoria Webster has cerebral palsy, and in this book, co-written with her mother Diana, her mother describes how she was bullied at school. For example "A smaller boy following her began to mimic her slight camel-like kick with one foot as she walked and another boy with him laughed and giggled" and

Her schoolmates used to play what they called Victoria-in-the-Cage. The game was for her classmates to put her in the middle and circle her with their desks. Gradually they pushed the desks closer and closer together and moved forwards, so that eventually she was forced to crawl under them to escape while they laughed and jeered at her.

Nevertheless, Victoria persevered with her schooling, and eventually qualified as a doctor and became a casualty consultant. But her mother writes that

I still feel she has been deeply scarred in one way. All the praise . . . of her undoubted skill or ability cannot even now quite remove her self-doubt and lack of complete confidence in herself . . . not because of her physical handicap . . . it is the result of other people's reactions to it.

Even just these two examples bring out many aspects of bullying. First, it can take different forms – we will look at these shortly. Second, it generally goes on over a period of time – the impact is cumulative. Third, the victim feels relatively powerless – perhaps because of being outnumbered, lacking confidence or, as in Victoria's case, having a disability or some other attribute that can be used to single them out. Fourth, the effects can be long-term. Victims of bullying can often overcome it, though not always – there have been suicides due at least in considerable part to being bullied (as we see in Chapter 4). But even in adulthood, former victims can have vivid memories of such experiences. For example, in a study of adult stammerers,[3] many recalled their experiences at school. One 36-year-old woman said:

> My school days have had a profound effect on my adulthood. The bullying has haunted me all my life. I sometimes have difficulty in staying in employment and often wonder if this could be an effect of the school bullying.

Fortunately we know a lot more now about school bullying than we did a generation ago. Also, this knowledge is beginning to pay off in terms of helping victims, preventing bullying, and devising effective intervention strategies at various levels – family, peer group, school, community. We will explore all this in the chapters to follow. But we should start with the issue of definition.

WHAT IS BULLYING? THE MATTER OF DEFINITION

Even if we think we can recognize bullying when we see it, we need as clear a definition as possible, if researchers are going to be able to carry out systematic studies (as described in Chapter 2). It is clear that bullying is a kind of aggressive behaviour, and aggression is usually defined in terms of an intent to cause harm. But equally clearly, not all aggression is bullying. For example I remember as a boy at school sometimes getting into a fight with a classmate. But if this happened just once or twice, and if we were fairly well matched in strength, this would not be bullying. It would only become bullying if one of us was clearly stronger, and then repeatedly attacked the other again and again.

This suggests two aspects that distinguish bullying as a particular form of aggression: it is repeated, and there is an imbalance of power. This concept of bullying was first put forward clearly by Dan Olweus, a Swedish psychologist who has worked in Norway for much of his career. As early as 1973 he wrote a book about 'school mobbing' in Swedish (translated into English in 1978 as *Aggression in Schools: Bullies and Whipping Boys*). However the connotations of *mobbing* (actually a Norwegian word similar to bullying) and old-fashioned terminology such as whipping boys, became clarified or changed by his 1993 book *Bullying at School: What we know and what we can do*.[4] This book was very influential. It has been translated into many languages, and helped push forward a great deal of research and action. Having said that, the 40 years since its publication has seen the development of an extensive research program and a vast amount of new knowledge being brought into the public domain.

The work of Olweus suggested a definition of bullying as repeated aggressive acts against someone who cannot easily defend themselves. The four main defining criteria are then:

- An action that harms or is likely to harm someone
- Done with intent to harm
  (these are criteria of aggression generally)
- Repeated over time
- With an imbalance of power such that the victim cannot easily defend himself or herself
  (these are criteria specific to bullying).

Another definition, which Sonia Sharp and I put forward in 1994, is that bullying is a 'systematic abuse of power'. This is succinct, and captures the main criteria.

The precise definition is still being argued over. Several current examples are shown in Table 1.1. The American Academy of Pediatrics definition and the Volk and colleagues definition does not include

Table 1.1 Some current definitions of bullying

Source	Definition
American Academy of Pediatrics stgove@aap.org	Bullying is unwanted, aggressive behaviour among school-aged children that involves a real or perceived power imbalance
Volk, Dane & Marini (2014)	Bullying is aggressive goal-directed behaviour that harms another individual within the context of a power imbalance.
US Centers for Disease Control and Prevention	Bullying is any unwanted aggressive behaviour(s) by another youth or group of youths who are not siblings or current dating partners that involves an observed or perceived power imbalance and is repeated multiple times or is highly likely to be repeated.
Department for Education, London, UK (2017)	Bullying is behaviour by an individual or group, repeated over time, that intentionally hurts another individual or group, either physically or emotionally. . . . Many experts say that bullying involves an imbalance of power between the perpetrator and the victim.
Dankmeijer / European Anti-Bullying Network (2017)	People are bullied when they are regularly exposed to policing actions with implicit or explicit intent to raise own or reduce others social status, and when it is difficult to defend themselves due to individual, social or cultural reasons.

repetition. The Centers for Disease Control and Prevention definition, arrived at after considerable consultation, does include repetition, but excludes sibling bullying and dating bullying. The Department for Education in London definition initially excluded the imbalance of power aspect, but the addendum that 'many experts say. . .' was added after representations by anti-bullying researchers. The Dankmeijer definition, presented to the European Anti-Bullying Network, refers to 'social and cultural reasons'. Here he intends to bring in the concept of social norms – what is considered normal and acceptable in a particular social or cultural context. For example, norms about homosexual behaviour have been negative in the past, although changing rapidly in western societies; and for example homophobic bullying, which is still widespread, would be explicitly covered by this definition.

Another debate is about whether bullying should be restricted to children (American Academy of Pediatrics, US Centers for Disease Control and Prevention), or not (the other definitions in Table 1.1). This matters if we want to discuss, for example, teacher-pupil or pupil-teacher bullying; or even workplace bullying. A further twist in this discussion of definitions comes when we consider cyberbullying. But to introduce that, let's look next at the different forms that bullying can take.

DIFFERENT FORMS OF BULLYING

The most obvious kind of bullying is physical – a larger child hits, punches or kicks a smaller one. Our knowledge of this has a long history. Thomas Hughes' (1857) book, Tom Brown's School Days, describes physical bullying by Flashman and his gang at Rugby school. This often consisted of putting boys in a blanket and tossing them violently: "What your bully really likes in tossing, is when the boys kick and struggle, or hold on to one side of the blanket, and so get pitched bodily on to the floor; it's no fun to him when no one is hurt or frightened" (p. 134). However bullying can also obviously be verbal – insults, threats, demeaning comments. In the two examples we started with, both verbal and physical bullying are evident. Physical bullying might also include damage to belongings, or the kind of desk-pushing ordeal that Victoria suffered. Verbal bullying might include extortion – demanding money or possessions with threats.

Through much of the twentieth century, aggression generally was described in terms of physical or verbal attacks. But in the 1980s and 1990s, several psychologists in Europe and North America drew attention to other kinds of aggression, which they called indirect, or relational. Indirect aggression is not face-to-face, but done by means of third parties – for example spreading nasty rumours about someone, or persuading others not to play with someone. Relational means actions which damage someone's reputation, and again nasty rumour spreading is a prime example. Bullying can take these forms too, so systematic social exclusion, and repeatedly spreading denigrating rumours about someone, count as additional forms of bullying. These four main types – physical, verbal, social exclusion, rumour-spreading – largely defined our knowledge of bullying through the twentieth century. This century however has seen the rise of what is very generally called cyberbullying. This refers to bullying by mobile phones and the internet. It has some special characteristics and we will look at it in more detail in a later section.

BULLYING IS AN INTERNATIONAL ISSUE

Serious research and consideration of school bullying started, in Europe at least, in the Scandinavian countries – especially Norway and Sweden, soon followed by Finland. This was in the 1970s and 1980s. In the 1990s, interest and concern developed rapidly in the UK, and soon many other European countries. Some of this was sparked, unfortunately, by suicides related to bullying. This had been the case in Norway, where in 1982 three boys aged 10–14 years, in different schools, committed suicide due to bullying in the space of a couple of weeks. The media interest in this, public concern and some prior research by Olweus suggesting the scale of the problem led to a Nationwide Campaign against Bullying in all 3,550 Norwegian schools.

In retrospect, this can be seen as a defining moment in the work on school bullying. It showed how a combination of events, media dissemination and research findings can lead to decisive social and political action. It undoubtedly inspired further work in much of Europe in the 1990s. The events have tragically often been suicides; the enormity and finality of a child taking his or her life, often leaving a note describing his or her continuing anguish and torment at being relentlessly bullied, can awaken fears in any parent and be difficult for politicians to ignore. However, events can also be survey findings; in England, I and colleagues carried out early surveys on the extent of bullying in 1990, and we found levels about twice those reported in Norway. This was taken up by the press as 'Is Britain the Bullying Capital of Europe?', soon becoming 'Britain is the Bullying Capital of Europe'. Such reports were instrumental in getting government funding for the first major intervention project in the UK. These and subsequent intervention projects are described in Chapter 6.

The work in Scandinavia and the UK also influenced researchers in Canada, Australia and New Zealand. Here too work commenced in the 1990s, and these countries have continued a very vigorous tradition of research and action. Quite separately from the work in Europe, there was a long tradition of work on bullying in Japan (where it is called *ijime*). This went back at least to the 1980s. It was only in the 1990s, partly due to international funding from UNESCO, that European, Australian and Japanese researchers got together to share experiences, and realize how much commonality there was – as well as some important differences (to be discussed shortly).

In the US, there had been a lot of work on peer aggression in the 1980s and 1990s, but it was the Columbine High School massacre in 1999, in which two students shot and killed 12 other students and a teacher, that led to an increase in concerns about bullying. The two student shooters had reportedly been bullied previously, and a 2000 report found that many premeditated school shootings could be linked to bullying. Although coming in somewhat later than researchers in many other countries, bullying is now a major research topic in the US, and it is the single largest contributing country in terms of research output.

Through the twenty-first century, school bullying has been picked up as an issue across the globe. There has been considerable work in South Korea, Hong Kong and Mainland China, Singapore and some other South-East Asian countries, and growing interest in South Africa and some other African countries, Arabic countries, South America, Russia and the Indian sub-continent.

Bullying has become recognized as a fundamental human rights issue. For children, it is a right to have schooling free of fear and intimidation. They should not have to put up with being bullied at school. This is documented by a United Nations report from 2016, *Ending the torment: tackling bullying from the schoolyard to cyberspace*, with contributions from countries across the globe.

But although bullying appears to be a common issue across the globe, is it really the same phenomenon in different countries?

BULLYING IN DIFFERENT COUNTRIES

The words *bully* or *bullying* are North European in origin; the Encarta World English Dictionary (1999) defines a *bully* as an aggressive person who intimidates or mistreats weaker people. It says that the origin is in the mid-sixteenth century, probably from Middle Dutch *boele* 'lover'. The meaning changed over the centuries to 'fine fellow', and then 'blusterer' or show-off – someone who displays his or her power. But this more positive meaning of bullying is still found in the phrase 'bully for you' or 'well done!'

In the Netherlands now, the word for *bullying* is *pesten* – quite evocative in English! In Scandinavian countries the word *mobbing* or *mobbning* is very similar. These words correspond well in meaning to English *bullying*, especially if *mobbing* does not necessarily imply a group context (that is, some bullying can be one-on-one).

But not all countries have similar words. In fact, the Latin languages in southern Europe do not have a close equivalent. They have words for aggression and violence, but not specifically for bullying. But they recognize the concept, and for example in Italy the term il bullismo is now widely used, while in Spain the actual word bullying has been adopted. The situation is somewhat similar in eastern Europe. In Russia there is no close equivalent; the word izdevatel'stvo has a profile quite similar to that of bullying, but it picks up physical and verbal types rather than social exclusion.

The choice of word for bullying is important, as it can affect how we measure it and how we make cross-national comparisons. For example, when I visited Qatar, I found that there and in some other Arabic countries the word tanamor (in English transliteration) is widely used. However tanamor literally means like a tiger, or tigerish, which gives a rather positive image of bullying. So there is a debate about which Arabic word is best to use here; an alternative word for bullying in Arabic might be esteqwa (in English transliteration) 'إستقواء', for example. Arab countries also use different terminologies for bullying according to their dialect (for example, in Egypt baltaja, 'بلطجة'; meaning hooligan or thug) and sometimes they use descriptive behaviour (e.g. name-calling, excluding, pushing, etc.) rather than a specific term for bullying.

We have seen how, in Japan, ijime is the term used to describe bullying. The leading researcher on bullying in Japan, Yohji Morita, has defined ijime as "A type of aggressive behaviour by which someone who holds a dominant position in a group-interaction process, by intentional or collective acts, causes mental and/or physical suffering to another inside a group". This is certainly similar to definitions of bullying, but it places more emphasis on the group process. In fact social exclusion would fit very well with this definition of ijime, and it does seem to be more prominent in Japan, and also in South Korea. In South Korea, the term wang-ta is widely used by children; wang means 'king' or 'big', and ta is a short version of ttadolim (isolation) or tadolida (to isolate). Thus, wang-ta stands for severe exclusion.

Japan and South Korea are more collectivistic societies, whereas European and North American societies are more individualistic. In collectivist societies, the group one is in has central importance; whereas in individualist societies, one has fewer close ties beyond the immediate family. Thus, if you want to hurt someone, social exclusion may be a particularly effective tactic in collectivist societies. And indeed, social exclusion seems to be more embedded in the idea of bullying in these countries.

HOW DO WE KNOW ABOUT THE DIFFERENT MEANINGS OF WORDS FOR BULLYING?

We can look up the meaning of words in dictionaries and, of course, that can be informative. But dictionaries reflect adult rather than child meanings and can be behind the times. For example, in South Korea the dictionary yields terms such as *gipdan-ttadolim* (group isolation), *gipdan-gorophim* (group harassment) or *hakkyo-pokryuk* (school violence). But as Hyojin Koo and later Seung-ha Lee showed, in practice children in South Korea nowadays use the more slang term, *wang-ta* – and even that is changing, with, more recently, the use of the term *jjin-ta*.[5] These are not terms used in adult discourse, but if we want to find out children's experiences, it may be best to use them.

We can ask children directly what they mean by terms such as *bullying, pesten, ijime, wang-ta* and so on. But for more precise and exact assessments, I and other colleagues designed a stick figure cartoon test. This uses stick figure cartoons, so they can be used across genders and across nationalities. We show a range of cartoons showing situations, many (but not all) of which can often be thought of as bullying (physical, verbal, relational, cyber . . .) but which do vary in terms of the criteria we discussed earlier – intent to harm, repetition, imbalance of power.

As an example, one cartoon shows a severe kind of social exclusion, shown in Figure 1.1, with the caption *No one wants to be with Julia for a paired activity*. This is a common situation in eastern countries, where children often pair up to tidy the classroom for the next lesson; but it can be understood anywhere. Pupils are asked "is this *bullying?*" (or *ijime, pesten, . . .*). (The name Julia is of course changed to one familiar in the country). In England 65% of pupils said it was *bullying*; but this rose to 76% in Japan (for *ijime*) and 85% in South Korea (for *wang-ta*).

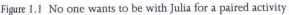

Figure 1.1   No one wants to be with Julia for a paired activity

Another example is shown in Figure 1.2. Here the caption is *The rest of the team won't let Millie take part in a competition, even though she is one of the best players, because she is from a lower year group.* Here 81% of English pupils said this was bullying. But this fell to 49% in South Korea who said this was *wang-ta,* and only 29% in Japan who said this was *ijime.* The probable explanation for this is that these eastern societies are more hierarchical. In terms of the cultural dimensions proposed by the Dutch social scientist Geert Hofstede, they are higher on a measure of power distance (defined as the extent to which less powerful members expect and accept that power is distributed unequally; there is more respect for older persons). Thus in Japan and South Korea, excluding a younger child, even when they are so good at the game, is justified.

These examples raise quite profound questions about what bullying means in different societies. Clearly what is considered acceptable behaviour – even if it is hurtful – varies in different societies. And of course some kinds of aggression (as in warfare) are considered legal and (by most people) justifiable, so this does

Figure 1.2 The rest of the team won't let Millie take part in a competition, even though she is one of the best players, because she is from a lower year group

complicate our definition. In fact the Australian psychologist Ken Rigby advocated an extended definition of bullying as "Bullying involves a desire to hurt + a harmful action + a power imbalance + (typically) repetition + an unjust use of power + evident enjoyment by the aggressor and generally a sense of being oppressed on the part of the victim".

CYBERBULLYING

Rigby's definition was proposed in his 2002 book, *New perspectives on bullying*. While new at the time, this book predated the widespread development and use of the internet and mobile phones, which came about in the next few years. By around 2008, smart phones that accessed the internet were becoming widely available, and their use spread rapidly amongst young people. Of course, these technological developments brought great opportunities and benefits; but there is also the dark side to these, and cyberbullying has been a prominent example of this.

What constitutes cyberbullying can be very varied. Some common examples are attacks and threats by text messages, emails or postings on social networking sites; denigration (put-downs); flaming (online verbal fights); cyberstalking (persistent online intimidation); exclusion (from an online group); masquerade (pretending to be someone else to send/post material to damage someone); outing (sharing embarrassing information or images of someone); being trolled in an online game and putting up false profiles and distributing personal material against someone's wishes.

A typical example comes from a report by Ditch the Label, a UK anti-bullying charity. One 13-year old girl is quoted as saying

> I was sent loads of horrible messages on several social media accounts, sent death threats with people telling me to kill myself. I also received phone calls and text messages attacking me. Furthermore, they were standing outside my house being abusive and saying horrible things to me. Fake accounts were made using my name to be horrible to others and to me.[6]

The word *cyberbullying* suggests that this is just another form of bullying – another way in which someone who gets enjoyment from hurting another (see Chapter 3) can do so. The quote from the 13-year old girl is an illustration of this. There is quite a lot of evidence that the children or young people involved in online or cyberbullying are often (but not always) the same as those involved in offline, or what is now often called traditional, bullying (i.e. direct physical and verbal attacks). Also the two kinds often appear to interlink; a playground attack may lead to retaliation online, and an online attack can result in a face-to-face confrontation the next day. However not all researchers agree with this conclusion, and some think that the differences between traditional and cyberbullying are very considerable, becoming more so as the internet plays a larger and larger part in young people's lives and as children get involved in this at ever younger ages.

Some of the distinctive features of cyberbullying have been known of and written about for a long time. One is particularly relevant when considering the motivation for bullying someone else. Cyber-bullying is primarily indirect rather than face-to-face; there is the possibility of the cyberbullies being 'anonymous' or 'invisible' if they try to hide their identity. This could reduce the risks involved (for example of retribution). In fact one theory about cyberbullying has been called 'the revenge of the nerds' – that it is an opportunity for a weaker child, bullied in the playground, to get his or her own back (in fact there is rather limited support for this view). On the other hand, the cyberbully does not usually see the victim's reaction, at least in the short-term. This could reduce the rewards the bully might hope to get, either by displaying his or her power to others or enjoying the suffering of the victim (see Chapter 3).

Two other distinctive features are more important when we con-sider the likely effects of being a cyber (compared to traditional) victim. One is that, in cyber attacks, the breadth of the potential audi-ence is increased. In the playground, your humiliation might be seen by a handful of onlookers; but in cyberspace, it could be hundreds or thousands of people who visit the website – potentially an almost unlimited number. The second is that cyberbullying is difficult to escape from; there is little or no respite. For traditional bullying at school, the evenings, weekends and holidays would provide a break; but cyber attacks could come at any time on your mobile phone, even at night. In theory you could avoid this by not using your mobile phone or the internet, but this would be drastic and unacceptable to the vast majority of young people nowadays. We will look at the relative impacts of traditional and cyber victimization in Chapter 4.

One definition of cyberbullying that I and colleagues have used is "an aggressive, intentional act carried out by a group or individual, using mobile phones or the internet, repeatedly and over time against a victim who cannot easily defend him or herself". This follows on from the standard definition. There is debate about whether it is appropriate to just carry over the definition in this way. Regarding the repetition criterion, it has often been pointed out that a single perpetrator act may be viewed or passed on many times by oth-ers, and that this could often be foreseen by the perpetrator – so it might be legitimate to count a single perpetrator act as cyberbullying. Regarding the imbalance of power criterion, the usual signs of this for traditional bullying – physical strength, social status, or numbers of bullies – do not so obviously apply, especially if the perpetrator withholds his or her identity. However, anonymity in itself may indicate an imbalance of power – the perpetrator knows the victim, but not vice versa; and if there is not anonymity and the victim does know who the perpetrator is, then the traditional criteria may still be relevant. These issues are still debated, with some researchers preferring to use the concept of cyber aggression more generally. However, much research has used the term *cyberbullying*.

2

FINDING OUT ABOUT BULLYING AND WHY
STATISTICS CAN BE MISLEADING

In Chapter 1 we looked briefly at the history of research on school bullying. There has actually been an enormous increase in the number of research articles on the topic during this century. There was just a trickle of articles up to the mid-1970s – the topic was virtually neglected. According to the ISI Web of Knowledge indexing service, the number of articles including the term bully in the title or abstract was just eight up to 1975. From 1976 to 1985 it was 60. From 1986 to 1995 it was 201. From 1996 to 2005 it was 1,546. From 2006 to 2015 it was 8,251. These totals do include articles on other kinds of bullying than school bullying, but the majority are on school bullying or on children and young people. There has clearly been a staggering increase in publications over the last 20 years. Recent years have seen something like three new articles every day – a challenge for researchers to keep up with what is being done!

An analysis I carried out with Fethi Berkkun on the topics of these articles shows that the majority are presenting empirical data of some kind; in other words, new information has been gathered through qualitative or quantitative methods, as explained shown in later sections. The remaining articles are reviews or opinion pieces, or sometimes meta-analyses. A meta-analysis is a statistical review of a large number of articles on a certain topic – for example on the effects of being a victim. Meta-analyses make sense once a large number of individual researches on a topic have been published, and a few examples will be considered later.

So what kinds of data are presented in this large number of empirical articles? The great majority present quantitative data, with a small minority presenting qualitative data (or occasionally, both). These two kinds of data have their own advantages and disadvantages; actually a mixed methods approach – combining the two – can sometimes be an excellent way forward.

QUALITATIVE METHODS

Researchers using qualitative methods do not use numerical analyses or statistics; rather, they rely on getting more narrative descriptions of experiences. Common methods used here are interviews and focus groups. Interviews could elicit the kinds of case study material we saw at the start of Chapter 1, of course in more detail. Generally, a qualitative researcher would collect a number of interviews. These are often what is called *semi-structured*; this means that there is a general framework of key questions to ask (such as 'have you been bullied?'), but also scope to ask follow-up questions or even unplanned for questions if new areas of interest get opened up.

Interview material can provide detailed information on how someone has experienced bullying, how they felt, what they did about it and what happened. It can also give insight into how things developed over time – how the bullying started, how it changed. Of course one can also interview the perpetrators of bullying, or witnesses of bullying, as well as victims. After a number of interviews have been collected, the researcher will usually carry out some kind of thematic analysis, to extract the important themes or messages coming from the transcripts.

For example, Elizabeth Nassem, a researcher at Birmingham City University, carried out individual and group semi-structured interviews about bullying with 9–11 year olds, and their teachers, in a junior school. She identified a number of themes from the interviews.

For example, one theme was *Why do children bully*. Of a number of relevant extracts, an example comes from 10-year-old Yana (all names are pseudonyms), who in an individual interview commented:

Yana: I think they can get a lot of respect from people around them and people eventually . . . they get a lot of friends because they're in power. Like when you're bullying people, other people around think, oh look, she has so much power, if I'm her friend she won't bully me, and she's strong so if anyone annoys me I can tell her this and that.

Another theme was *Punishment*. The following extract from an interview with Sidra, also 10 years old, was coded under both this theme and the previous *Why do children bully* theme:

Interviewer: So there are different ways of dealing with bullying, like punishing the bully, helping those who. . .
Sidra: Punishing the bully is not going to do anything, because that bully's got punished now and you know what that bully's going to do to that other person, try and hit them. That's happened before, I've seen it.
Interviewer: Or helping the bullies learn about how to understand other people's feelings.
Sidra: Bullies don't understand other people's feelings. They think that no-one has feelings except for them. Some bullies bully people because something's happened with them, like something's wrong with them.

Even just these short examples show how perceptive some children can be. But clearly Yana and Sidra may have somewhat different views on why children bully. Group interviews or focus groups provide another option for qualitative researchers. Here, the researcher assembles a small group of perhaps four, six or eight young people together to discuss a topic such as bullying. Focus groups provide less confidentiality – a victim might be less willing to open up about his or

her experiences, for example – but a possible advantage is that you can see a range of opinions from the different focus group members. They may challenge or disagree with each other, or they may prompt each other to reveal other ideas that might not come from individual interviews.

For example, Elizabeth Nassem carried out a focus group with five children from the junior school. The discussion got on to racist bullying:

Interviewer: So who gets bullied for their skin colour?
Aailia: Loads of people.
Yana: It's like saying, black, black, black.
Interviewer: So if you're dark you get bullied?
Aailia: Not only if you're dark, if you're light skinned, if you're fair skinned.
Taaliq: It depends which person you're bullying. If it's someone who's not that light skinned. . . . Someone who's light skinned they will target the people who are brown and black, but if there's someone who is black then they're targeting people who are white and brown. But it's not every single person who is doing it, only some.

Here the discussion prompts Taaliq to make a very perceptive comment that might not come from an individual interview. The next extract shows how children may challenge each other's views:

Tayyub: One thing I don't like is when the teachers say, if something like that happens call a teacher, they don't do anything.
Aailia: Yeah, but that teacher did something.

In these interviews, children are talking about recent events. Interviews can also be retrospective, looking back on one's time at school. In Chapter 1, the recollection of an adult of being bullied at school because of their stammer, is an example from such a retrospective interview.

There are other ways of getting qualitative data too. For example, young people can be asked to draw pictures of their experiences, or take photographs to illustrate their feelings of different place in school (a technique called *photostory*).[1] Another way of getting information from young people themselves is to use *quality circles* (described further in Chapter 6); these are problem-solving groups of pupils who spend perhaps one lesson a week, for a term, researching a topic such as 'what to do about bullying', reaching conclusions and recommendations, and reporting back to the class or the school.

QUANTITATIVE METHODS

The majority of research studies, however, have used quantitative methods – essentially, getting numerical data and often using statistics to see how generalizable the findings are. The two main methods have been questionnaire surveys and peer nominations.

Questionnaire surveys are the most common way of getting information about bullying. Usually, these questionnaires are given to children or young people, to report their own experiences – what are called *self-report* questionnaires. The questionnaire will often start with a definition of what bullying is, and then ask if they have experienced being bullied. Usually some time period is mentioned, for example

How often have you been bullied in the past couple of months?

The respondent is then given a list of alternatives to choose one from – for example 'I haven't been bullied', or 'only once or twice', or 'several times', or 'about once a week' or 'several times a week'. When the questionnaire is given as a survey to a large number of young people, this will give a percentage figure for those who are victims of bullying (perhaps not counting the 'only once or twice' responses if repetition over time is thought to be an important part of defining bullying).

A questionnaire like this will typically go on to ask other questions, such as what type of bullying was experienced, where it happened, how many other children or young people were involved, what the victim did, whether they told anyone, whether any action was taken. It may also ask about if they have witnessed others being bullied; or if they have taken part themselves in bullying others.

An early questionnaire along these lines was developed by Dan Olweus in the 1980s. Called the *Olweus Bully/Victim Questionnaire*, it has been widely used and updated this century to include cyberbullying.[2] However there are many other questionnaires available, and often researchers design their own questionnaire with a specific purpose in mind. Such questionnaires were initially paper based, but increasingly are now filled in online.

Larger-scale surveys

Surveys are usually carried out in one country. Many are small scale, but some are on a more national basis. For example, in England, the government-sponsored Tellus surveys were designed to give annual nationwide figures on issues around child well-being, including questions on bullying. Tellus 1 and Tellus 2 were pilots and small scale, but the Tellus 3 National Report, carried out in spring 2008, provided data from nearly 149,000 pupils at years 6, 8 and 10 (approx. 11, 13 and 15 years old) across 145 Local Authorities. It found that 14% of 8–16 year olds were bullied in school at least once in the last 4 weeks, and 8% were bullied somewhere else.

Tellus 4 was carried out in late 2009; it reported on data from over 253,000 pupils in the same year groups, from 3,699 schools and a total of 253,755 children across England.[3] It included a section on bullying, which started with a definition:

> We'd like to ask you about bullying. Bullying can mean lots of different things to different people. Bullying is when people hurt or pick on you on purpose, for example by teasing you, hitting or kicking you or saying that they will do this. It can involve people taking or breaking your things, making you do something you don't want to do, leaving you out or spreading hurtful and

untrue rumours. Bullying can be face to face, by mobile phone or on the internet.

After this definition, the young person was asked if he or she had ever been bullied at school; and if so, whether it was more than one year ago/in the last year/in the last six months/in the last four weeks, and whether this had happened a few times this year/every month/ every week/most days/every day. The children were similarly asked about being bullied when not in school (including on the journey to school). Altogether, 48% of young people said they had experienced bullying at some point in school, and 21% said they had experienced it out of school.

The figure of 48% is high – nearly one-half of pupils were bullied! But, this figure varied greatly with the time frame (how long ago the bullying happened). The 48% refers to if pupils had ever been bullied at school. This falls to 25% who had been bullied in the last year, 13% who had been bullied in the last month and 9% who had been bullied in the last 4 weeks. It is also worth noting that the definition used, given previously, although it covers a good range of behaviours, does not mention the imbalance of power criterion; thus, depending on pupil's understanding of 'bullying', some behaviours not involving an imbalance of power may also have been picked up.

The survey found no differences in victim experiences between boys and girls. Victim prevalence was higher in younger children, in children with disabilities and in White rather than Asian or Black British pupils. Unfortunately the Tellus surveys were then discontinued, and even Tellus 3 and Tellus 4 had some procedural differences, so they cannot give us a picture of time trends in England nationally.

A more recent survey, across the whole of the UK, was reported by the charity DitchtheLabel.[4] They sampled 10,020 young people aged 12–20 years. This survey did not give a definition of bullying. It is stated that "the very nature of bullying is subjective, meaning that everybody has a different idea of the behaviours that carer considered to be bullying". They therefore asked about six kinds of experiences such as "have you ever physically attacked somebody?" or "have you ever said something nasty to someone online?". Not surprisingly, these kinds of questions produce large victim figures; in this survey, 54% said they had been 'bullied' (experienced one of these six behaviours) at some point, and 20% said they had been bullied at least once a week. However these figures may include fights and conflicts between equals that would not usually be considered as bullying.

In the United States, some nationwide statistics come from the School Crime Supplement to the National Crime Victimization Survey.[5] This was carried out with 12–18 year olds across the US and students were asked if another student had bullied them during the school year, mentioning seven kinds of attack. The definition provided was that from the US Centers for Disease Control and Prevention given in Table 1.1. Altogether, from 2,317 respondents, 20.8% reported being a victim. Of these however, two-thirds said it had only happened once or twice in the school year; so the figure falls to 6.9% who were victims for at least once or twice a month. Black and other ethnic groups were victims most, and Asian and Hispanic least. As is commonly found, victim rates were slightly higher in girls than boys, and decreased with age/grade.

Cross-national surveys

A number of surveys have attempted cross-national comparisons, giving the same questionnaire to young people in a range of countries across the globe. This can result in 'league-tables' of countries which are apparently doing well or poorly in terms of, for example, being a victim of school bullying. Some main surveys of this kind are summarized in Table 2.1. All of these surveys are gathering self-reported data from children and young people. Some measure bullying perpetration, and all measured being a victim of bullying.

Ostensibly then, despite some variations in definition, procedure and time reference period, these surveys are measuring the same thing. Unfortunately, there are some clear anomalies! A glaring example comes from comparing figures for Sweden from the EU Kids Online (EUKO) and Health Behaviour of School-aged Children (HBSC)

Table 2.1 Some main cross-national surveys of victim rates (from pupil self-report)

Survey	Countries covered	Dates of survey	Ages of children/ young people
Health Behaviour of School-aged Children (HBSC)	Around 40, mostly European but also US, Canada, Russia.	Every 4 years starting in 1993/94	11, 13 and 15 years
EU Kids Online (EUKO)	25 European countries	2010	9–16 years
Global School Health Survey (GSHS)	About 80 mainly developing countries	Irregular basis	13 to 17 years
Trends in International Mathematics and Science Study (TIMSS)	About 60 countries	Every 4 years from 1995	4th grade (9–10 years) and 8th grade (about 13– 14 years)
Programme for International Student Assessment (PISA)	52 countries	2015 (earlier years did not include pupil data on bullying)	15 years

surveys. In the EUKO data from 2010, Sweden comes fourth equal highest (4/25) for victim rates – they seem to be doing poorly. But in the HBSC data from 2009/10 (well-matched for survey period), Sweden came third from lowest (36/38)! So Sweden was doing well. Scientifically, this is not satisfactory. The other surveys too show only modest agreement when comparing countries – the different 'league tables' (where countries overlap in surveys) do not agree very well.[6]

There are a variety of reasons why these surveys might disagree. These include the following: what kind of definition is used, what kinds of bullying were mentioned or asked about, what time period is being referred to, what kind of samples were used, whether dropout rates were appreciable and how questions (including the term bully-ing when used) were translated into different languages. At present, unfortunately, it is difficult to really say which countries are doing well and which are doing not so well in terms of prevalence rates.

Peer nominations

The main alternative method for quantitative researchers is peer nominations. Here, each pupil in the class fills in a kind of questionnaire (or are interviewed) to ask them who gets bullied in their class (usually with a roster of names so they can check those they think are bullied). Sometimes they are asked to nominate perpetrators of bullying too, or other roles such as defenders. This of course does raise more ethical issues than most other methods, especially if children confer afterwards about how they have labelled others. However usually children have a pretty good idea of what bullying is going on anyway, and, so far, research suggests that if proper precautions are taken, including emphasizing the confidentiality of responses, then there need be no adverse effects.

Because peer nominations get information from most or all children in the class, it could be considered more reliable than self-report. That is for two reasons. One is simply numbers; if most children in the class independently agree that X is a victim, this may carry more weight than just one child's own view. Second, some children may not report accurately about themselves. In one study, in the US, Jaana Juvonen and colleagues compared self-reports and peer nominations of being a victim in 400 children aged 12–13 years.[7] They found that for 56% of the sample, there was agreement that a pupil was not a victim, and for 14% there was agreement that the pupil was a victim. But this left 30% of pupils where there was disagreement! For 23%, the pupil self-reported being a victim, but peers did not nominate him or her this way; these children were labelled 'paranoids'. For the remaining 7%, the pupil did not report being a victim, but most peers did nominate him or her in this role; these pupils were called 'deniers'. These labels, given by the researchers, do suggest that the peers are more 'correct' than the self-report nominations, and that may well be the case, but of course a pupil does have unique insight into his or her own situation, and it is possible (for example) that a former victim might still be labelled that way in the peer group, even if he or she has not been bullied for some period previously. One lesson from all this is that there are different perspectives on 'truth', and that using more than one method may be advisable in carrying out a research project.

The peer nomination procedure is rather more time-consuming than a traditional self-report survey, although specifically designed online programs can make it relatively fast. However it has most often been used on a class basis. An elaboration of the procedure, particularly developed by Rene Veenstra and colleagues in the Netherlands,[8] has been called *social network analysis*. Here, pupils also nominate who bullies who (or who defends who, etc). This allows a much more detailed analysis of, for example, how much cross-gender bullying there is, whether bullies attack a particular victim or a number of victims, whether bullies may also sometimes defend their friends and so on.

other methods

Of course there are other ways of getting quantitative data. Surveys, or nomination procedures, can be given to teachers, or parents, for example. These can be valuable, and for young children (up to say 7 or 8 years), for whom written questionnaires will be challenging, teacher nominations may be a preferred method. But especially for older children, and if we are researching peer bullying in school, it is really the pupil him- or herself, and the peer group, that know what is happening.

On a cross-national basis, for some time the PISA survey (see Table 2.1) used teacher reports about the extent of bullying in schools; but this now uses pupil reports. Teacher reports may be influenced by social desirability, especially when gathered in some official capacity. This was shown by experiences in Japan. Through the 1980s and into the 1990s, the Ministry of Education in Japan (Monbusho) published an *Annual fact-find on problem behaviour in school*, including incidents of bullying or ijime, as reported by teachers. These showed a rather steady decline over a number of years. Unfortunately, in the 1990s, quite a number of suicides occurred due to ijime (see Chapter 4). It was realized that the problem of ijime had not really decreased but was as serious as ever, and that pupil reports would be a more valid measure.

There are other methods entirely. Incident reports kept in schools can be useful, especially when examining changes over time in that school (perhaps after new procedures or interventions are put in place); but, due to varying methodologies, may not be very suitable for comparing different schools or gathering large-scale data. The cartoon test described in Chapter 1 is another quantitative kind of method, but is mainly suited to probing what kinds of behaviours pupils think that bullying (or harassment, teasing, ijime, etc.) is, rather than how frequent they are.

RELIABILITY AND VALIDITY OF ASSESSMENTS

Whether methods are qualitative or quantitative, it is desirable that findings are reliable and valid. Reliability means that another researcher using the same methods should come up with similar findings. Validity means that the conclusions drawn should be correct and should hold beyond just the very particular circumstances or sample of the study – that they have some generalizability.

In qualitative methods, a measure of reliability can be reached by showing the themes arrived at, or conclusions reached, back to the original participants (interviewees), and seeing if they feel these conclusions accord with their own experiences. Another measure would be to assess *saturation*; this means that enough data has been gathered, such that carrying out more interviews, or focus groups, no longer introduces new themes or changes the conclusions appreciably. A measure of validity can be arrived at by seeing if the themes and conclusions are recognized by other persons not part of the original sample (but to whom generalization is desired – for example pupils or teachers in other schools, or other parts of the country).

In quantitative studies, reliability can be assessed by splitting the sample in half and seeing if similar numerical figures (such as the prevalence of bullying) are arrived at. (Unsurprisingly, this is called *split-half reliability*). When quantitative comparisons are involved – for example comparing ages, or genders, or measures over time – statistical tests can be used. Essentially these will tell you if the sample you have is large enough, and the differences consistent enough, that if you were to repeat the study on a similar sample, or extend your sample, you would reach the same conclusion.

If there is only 1 chance in 20 that the finding would not be replicated on a similar sample, it is generally considered to have statistical significance. This is expressed as $p < .05$ (p, the probability of this finding being just a chance one, is less than 5 in 100 or 1 in 20).

Significance levels are considered as something of holy writ among many quantitative researchers. Often, findings will only be considered worth reporting if $p < .05$. For example, suppose victim rates are being compared in boys and girls, and the statistical test shows $p < .05$, then this will be reported as a definite finding: "boys were victimized more than girls". But suppose the test found that $p > .05$ (so there is a greater than 5 in 100, or 1 in 20, chance that the finding would not be replicated in a similar sample. The researcher will then often report: "no differences were found in victim rates between boys and girls". The .05 level for statistical significance is a conventional one, and a cautious researcher may prefer $p < .01$ (1 in 100) or more. On the other hand, someone desperate for results may take $p < .10$ (1 in 10 chance of not being replicated) as an interesting trend.

There are a number of problems in the way such findings are often reported, using statistics in this kind of way, and it helps to be aware of them when reading reports:

- The $p < .05$ or 1 in 20 criterion is clearly arbitrary. A finding significant at $p < .05$ might still be a fluke result, even if the chances of this are small. In fact, a fairly common problem here is if a researcher makes many comparisons on the same data set. They might compare males and females on different kinds of victimization, different kinds of roles and so on. Suppose they make 20 such comparisons. They highlight one 'significant' finding. But at $p < .05$, one can expect one 'significant' result out of 20 comparisons to be a chance finding, not replicable. There are statistical corrections that can be applied to allow for this, but often these corrections are not made.

- A second problem is that if the finding is not significant at $p < .05$, the researcher may be tempted to say that there is no difference (e.g. in victim rates for boys and girls). This is probably not a true conclusion; they will almost always have found some difference in victim rates, it is just that they cannot be very confident that it will replicate.

- A third problem is that, for large samples, even a quite small difference will be statistically significant; but it may be unimportant. Suppose we compare two high schools with say 2,000 pupils each; in one, 7.5% of pupils report being bullied, in the other, 7.3%. This might be statistically significant at $p < .05$, but the actual prevalence difference of 0.2% is really so small as to be unimportant. This has led to calls for *effect sizes* to be reported, as being as important (or more so) than conventional significance levels. The effect size refers to the size of the difference relative to the overall mean level (here, 0.2 compared to the mean of 7.4).

Ethical issues in assessments

Bullying is a sensitive topic, and asking about experiences of being bullied, especially, might bring up unpleasant memories and cause distress. There are also particular issues around consent where children and young people are concerned. In most countries, and certainly in the UK and US, any research will be carefully screened by an institutional ethics committee; it will not be able to proceed without their approval.

The kinds of issues an ethics committee will examine include the following:

- Is there informed consent? This should come from the young people themselves (so far as possible for their age), their parents/carers and teachers if in school settings. Informed consent means agreeing, knowing what kind of questions will be asked and what precautions will be taken.
- Will it be made clear that participation is voluntary, that questions can be left unanswered if desired, and that someone can withdraw their participation at any time if they wish to do so?
- Will the data be confidential, such that no child can be individually identified in any report or publication? However there should be a caveat here, in that if the researcher becomes aware of serious harm to some specific person which is recent or ongoing, and about which no action has been or is being taken, then outside help must be sought; the participant who has revealed information would be involved in deciding who to tell, and how, but not on the decision to tell.
- Will help be available should anyone be distressed? This might be having a school counsellor available, for example. Also, a help sheet with detailed websites and telephone help-lines can be provided to all participants.

In practice, difficulties do not often arise in carrying out these kinds of studies, but these kinds of precautions are sensible and usually mandatory.

DIFFERENT METHODS: THE PROS AND CONS

It will be clear by now that each method of study has advantages and disadvantages. The choice will depend on the kinds of questions the researcher is most interested in, as well as his or her disciplinary background. A mixture of methods may often be most fruitful, but will be more time-consuming and is relatively seldom attempted.

Qualitative methods are most useful for finding out the characteristics of a phenomenon. Even if we think we know about bullying from our own school days, things may be different for other kinds of pupils, in other schools, in other countries and at other times. An obvious example is cyberbullying. Contemporary adults will not have experienced this at school. An initial phase of qualitative study could be useful to establish the kinds of cyberbullying going on, before proceeding to a quantitative survey. A problem with going to quantitative surveys too quickly, could be that such surveys have predetermined questions or categories. You only get answers to the questions you ask and may miss out on important things you did not ask about. However, qualitative methods might also be useful after a quantitative survey in order to interpret particular findings. For example, suppose a gender difference is found for a certain type of bullying, then why is this the case? Interviews or focus groups might give useful insights.

However qualitative studies are usually on rather small samples, and do not give a general picture at a population level. Quantitative studies are most useful for establishing prevalence rates and for examining differences between groups or subgroups. Prevalence rates are important for social and political reasons. Showing that the experiences of being bullied are widespread, and not just for a tiny minority, is important in raising public awareness and prompting action about it (see Chapter 1). Comparing rates over time (in the same or similar populations) is important for seeing if such actions or interventions are having any success. Comparing groups – such as male/female, older/younger or by ethnicity or disability for example – is important for finding out which groups are most at risk (see Chapter 3), and for which kinds of bullying, and tailoring interventions accordingly (see Chapter 6).

However, studies need to be done with care, and conclusions also drawn carefully. This may be clear from looking at the surveys mentioned earlier in this chapter. Victim figures from 14% to 54% could be drawn from these – a wide range – and some surveys give even higher or even lower figures. A lot depends on what definition of bullying is used (or if one is used at all); what types of bullying are being assessed; what time period is being asked about (ever? the last school year? The last term?); how frequently it has happened (just once or twice? many times?); the characteristics of the sample and the extent of non-response or withdrawal rates. If someone asks whether pupils have experienced any kind of attack, at least once, over the last year, they will get high figures to report; if instead they ask if someone has been bullied (repeatedly and with a power imbalance) more than just once or twice during the last month, the figures will be much lower. The lesson is to interpret statistics with care and check out the methodology being used.

3

WHO BULLIES? WHO GETS BULLIED?

We saw in the previous chapter how prevalence figures for bullying vary greatly, depending on how you measure it. Nevertheless, most surveys, most of the time, suggest that it is a minority of children or young people who are involved – in one way or another. The majority of children can be classed as basically 'non-involved'. So, who are those who do get involved?

There are two important points to make here. The first is that anyone might get involved at some time or another. In my more detailed academic book on bullying,[1] I recounted how I personally had been both a victim, but also had taken part in bullying someone else, during my time at school. I guess in fact that a majority of readers might be in the same position. However only a smaller minority might have been involved systematically, or over a long time period. In other words, we are looking at degrees of involvement, not a black-and-white issue.

The second point is that we should not just be thinking about bullies and victims. There is actually a spectrum of different kinds of involvement – what has been called *participant roles* in bullying. We will look at this issue next.

PARTICIPANT ROLES IN BULLYING

The standard questionnaires and surveys on bullying, such as those described in Chapter 2, always ask about whether the respondent has been bullied – so, are they or have they been a *victim*? Many of these questionnaires also ask if the respondent has been a perpetrator, or taken part in bullying others – so, are they or have they been a *bully*? These are the two obvious roles in bullying. In light of the first point – that almost all of us may have been involved at some time or another – it may be unfortunate to label particular children as *victims* or *bullies* – it may even be counter-productive if we want to change behaviours – but it can be useful when doing research, if we want to find out the characteristics of those often involved in being victimized, or bullying others, or what the *risk factors* are. Here risk factors refer to what other factors (for example, family environment) might be associated with, or predict involvement in, these roles. We will look at these shortly. But first, let's look at what are the other participant roles.

Another category will clearly be the *not-involved* children. These will be those (usually the majority) who are nether victims, nor bullies, by the criteria we have chosen to use. We will see in a moment how they can be split further into different sub-categories. And a fourth category will be those who are both victims and bullies. These are generally referred to as the *bully-victims*. They may self-report, or be peer-nominated into, both these categories. They may be picked on by others, but also be perceived as provocative or annoying such that others may perceive them as also being bullying in their behaviour.

The origin of the term *participant roles* stems from the research of a Finnish psychologist, Christina Salmivalli. Besides the roles looked at previously, she split up the bully role (into three sub-roles) and the non-involved role (into two or three).[2] The victim role can also be split.

Bully sub-roles: here the three roles sometimes distinguished are *ringleader bully, assistant* and *reinforcer*. From this perspective, bullying is a group process – several people are involved. Although some bullying might be just one-on-one, more usually others are involved to some extent. The ringleader bully is then seen as the person who takes the lead, initiating the bullying. The assistant is someone who 'follows the leader', joining in with the bullying. The reinforcer is someone who does not join in directly, but provides more passive approval of the bullying by laughing or encouraging the bullies. These three roles are clearly different conceptually, although much research does suggest a lot of overlap between them.

Non-involved sub-roles: other children may see the bullying going on, but do not like it and do not reinforce it by laughing or encouraging it. At the most prosocial end, some children can be classed as *defenders*. They may challenge the bullies, perhaps telling them to stop; or comforting the victim; or getting help, perhaps from a teacher. Clearly the defender role is very important when school-based interventions against bullying are planned (see Chapter 6). Other children may just watch silently and do nothing. They are usually classed as *bystanders*, although some researchers argue that even passive onlooking (i.e. not intervening or defending) is in itself a form of reinforcement of the bullying. Finally, some children may be genuinely unaware of the bullying – the *outsiders*.

Victim sub-roles: the victim role is often split into *passive victims* and *provocative victims*. This distinction was used a lot by a Swedish psychologist, Anatol Pikas, where it was an important aspect of his Pikas Method of tackling bullying (see Chapter 6). The passive victim refers to a child or young person who has done nothing to provoke or justify the attacks made on them. The term *passive victim* is perhaps unfortunate, as it carries some negative connotation; the child may not be passive in any general sense. But the contrast is with the provocative victim, who is annoying in some ways to peers and may do things that are likely to result in attacks. For example they may barge into games inappropriately, or react aggressively to what others saw as a harmless joke. As can be seen, the provocative victim is rather similar to the bully-victim role described previously, and indeed the two roles overlap considerably. Pikas thought the distinction important, in that for passive victims the emphasis should entirely be on changing the behaviours of the bullies; whereas for provocative victims, it would be important to change the behaviours of the bullies *and* of the victim.

Having described the various roles, what has research found out about them – what are the likely predictors, or risk factors, for being in a certain role? Here, it will help to make use of what has been called the ecological model.[3]

THE ECOLOGICAL MODEL

The ecological model of human development, described by the US psychologist Urie Bronfenbrenner, is illustrated in Figure 3.1. It places the individual at the centre of a series of circular rings. Moving out, these rings indicate closer or more distant spheres of influence on the individual. In the next ring are those persons that he or

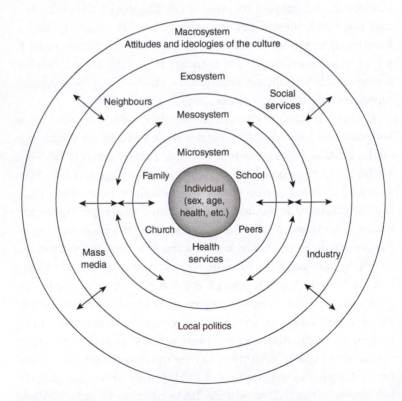

Figure 3.1 The ecological model, designed by Urie Bronfenbrenner[4]

she has immediate contact with, such as family, or peers in school; these are called microsystems. The next ring illustrates how microsystems might interact with each other on the child, for example how the quality of the child's home environment might affect his or her school performance or confidence with peers; this area is called the mesosystem. Moving out again are settings in which the child does not participate directly, but that do have an effect on the individual, for example, the work environment that a parent has may affect their behaviour at home and thus the child; this is called the exosystem. Finally we come to the general organization of social institutions in the society that the child is in, so for example how working hours, or unemployment (and perhaps social stigma attached to unemployment), affect parental stress; this area is called the macrosystem.

Bronfenbrenner emphasized the interactions amongst these different layers of influence, but at a simple level we can just consider the direct effect of individual factors, family factors, peer group factors, school factors, and wider society influences. Most investigated are the individual, family and peer group factors, and it makes sense to look at most of these separately for each of the main participant roles. After that we will look at the individual factors of age, and gender, and then at the school and society factors, more generally.

WHAT DO WE KNOW ABOUT CHILDREN OR YOUNG PEOPLE LIKELY TO BULLY OTHERS?

The early work by Dan Olweus in Sweden and Norway suggested that children who bullied others were hot-tempered and easily angered. They had a positive attitude toward violence, perhaps in part because some of them experienced violence in the home environment (from or between parents or siblings). However Olweus challenged the view that these children were fundamentally insecure or lacked self-esteem.

There are mixed views on the self-esteem of children who bully. It may depend on how self-esteem is measured. For example one well-known scale of self-esteem, by Susan Harter,[5] measures global self-worth, as well as specific aspects of self-esteem: scholastic competence, social acceptance, athletic competence, physical appearance and behavioural conduct. Children who bully may score low on scholastic competence (they may be disaffected from school) and behavioural conduct (they know their behaviour is not approved of!), but score quite high on social acceptance and athletic competence. It has also been argued that these children are high on what is called *defensive egotism*; this means, not that they have low self-esteem, but that they react angrily to minor threats to self-esteem. They would take offence easily, in line with Olweus' view of them having a hot-tempered personality.

Another area of discussion has been whether if children who bully do so from a lack of social skills. Perhaps they misread signals from others, and need help in understanding others' emotions? But on the whole, this view is not well supported. Rather, children who bully others do seem to show *moral disengagement*. This describes how someone can avoid the normal kinds of reasoning which would hold us back from hurting another person; these common processes are called cognitive restructuring (seeing the attack as justified – 'he deserved it'), minimizing one's role ('I didn't start it'), disregarding or distorting the consequences ('it was just for fun') or blaming the victim ('he started it').

Relatedly, children who bully often are found to be low on empathy. Two kinds of empathy are often distinguished – *affective empathy* and *cognitive empathy*. Affective empathy refers to how one in some way shares, or is affected by, the emotions of another – if they are sad, we too feel sad or at least feel sorry for them. Cognitive empathy is the understanding of someone's emotional state without necessarily sharing it – we understand someone is sad, but it does not affect us in the same way. Although the evidence is a bit mixed, most studies suggest that bullying children are low on affective empathy, but are not low on cognitive empathy.

A similar perspective on this has come from studies of *theory of mind*. The theory of mind concept refers to the understanding we have that someone else may feel differently from us, or think differently, or have different knowledge or opinions from us – in other words, a theory about other's minds. It is a kind of social skill. If we thought of bullies as lacking social skills, then we might expect them to do badly on tasks that measure these theory of mind abilities. But this is not the case. Most studies find bullying children do well on theory of mind tasks, with some studies finding that ringleader bullies do especially well.[6]

This set of findings led many researchers to think of bullies as having cold cognition; they can understand things well, but don't have affective empathy for their victims. In fact a good theory of mind might be helpful for ringleader bullies – they would know how best to hurt a victim and get a reaction from them, how to manage the peer group situation to maximize their social support and how to avoid detection from adults. Having said that, this may be more true of ringleader bullies than assistants or reinforcers. One study in the Netherlands of 13 year olds[7] used measures of social intelligence (it included items such as 'I can predict other people's behavior' which could be used to assess theory of mind). The findings suggested there were three kinds of pupils who were peer-nominated as bullies. One group was popular and socially intelligent; a second group was relatively popular and with average social intelligence scores; a third group, the smallest numerically, was unpopular and had lower than average scores on social intelligence. This study did not distinguish ringleader, assistant and reinforcer bullying roles, but it does suggest that a subset of popular bullies (perhaps more likely to be ringleaders) are high on social intelligence and theory of mind type abilities.

Some research in behaviour genetics has suggested that there is some heritable aspect to being likely to bully others. The main evidence comes from a study of of 1,116 families with same-sex twins, born in England and Wales during 1994–1995.[8] The researchers compared monozygotic (genetically identical) and dizygotic (non-identical) twins; if one twin is involved in bullying, is the other one? If there is greater agreeement, or concordance, in this for monozygotic twins, this suggests a genetic influence; if not, it suggests mainly environmental influence. In fact this study suggested quite strong heritability.

This does not mean that certain children are born to bully others! What it may mean is that some characteristics, such as poor emotional regulation, hot-tempered personality, impulsivity and sensation seeking, are partially heritable traits that could enhance the risk or likelihood of getting involved in bullying. Some studies have also linked bullying to Machiavellianism (thinking that other people are untrustworthy, and can be manipulated in dealings with them), psychopathy (impulsive, thrill-seeking behaviour, with low empathy, low anxiety) and callous-unemotional traits (lack of guilt, lack of empathy and callous use of others for one's own gain), all of which have some degree of heritability and may facilitate bullying.

However the environment certainly influences bullying behaviour. Several studies have suggested that poor communication with parents, and any bullying behaviour in the home (whether between parents, or parent to child, or with siblings) is associated with bullying behaviour in school. In addition, studies in Finnish classrooms have shown that bullying is more likely when the peer group in the class has more pro-bullying attitudes (or attitudes negative to victims), and bullying is less likely when there are more defenders in the class.[9]

In summary, children who get involved in bullying are not all of the same kind. Many tend to be impulsive and hot-tempered, easily taking offence. They may lack empathic feelings for others' hurt, and use strategies of moral disengagement; but they can be quite clever in terms of manipulating others and getting their own way. It is increasingly recognized that children who bully may get some payoff for their actions. This might be in terms of extorting money or possessions; but mainly, it is thought to be in terms of establishing and maintaining a dominant position in the peer group, and, in adolescence at least, appearing powerful and desirable to the (usually) opposite sex. This has been termed the *dominance hypothesis*. It is consistent with findings that although bullying children may not be especially liked by many others, they are often seen as powerful and having high status. Of course this need not be the case, and the extent to which this is so will depend too on school factors and school climate (see later section).

WHAT DO WE KNOW ABOUT CHILDREN OR YOUNG PEOPLE WHO ARE LIKELY TO BE BULLIED?

Again the early work of Dan Olweus gave a picture of those at risk of being victims, in this case being rather shy, anxious or cautious children who tend to submit when attacked. They may be rather poor in some social skills such as making and keeping friends, regulating emotions and responding assertively to provocations. They tend to be unpopular in the peer group.

In addition, there is fairly consistent evidence that victims tend to have low self-esteem. In fact, there is evidence here for what is called a *transactional model* between being a victim, and low self-esteem. What this means is that someone with low self-esteem is more vulnerable to being bullied, but also that being bullied results in lower self-esteem – a vicious circle.

Just as with children who bully, being a victim has also been found to have some heritability by behaviour genetic studies. Again, it is much too facile to say that there is a gene for being a victim. Rather, heritability probably works through factors such as introverted personality and poor social skills and emotion regulation.

The support (or lack of support) from peers can make a big difference. Whatever other risk factors are involved, if a child or young person has some good friends this will make bullying less likely. This does depend on the friends being trustworthy – they will stand by you rather than vanish when the bullies appear; and it helps if the friends have some reasonably high status in the peer group, rather than also being victims. These findings are borne out too by the research on defenders (see later).

Family factors can also be predictive of being a victim. Supportive, involved and communicative parents – or what is called *positive parenting* – is a protective factor; the children of such parents are less likely to be victims. However involvement can go too far. What has been called *over-protective parenting* has been rather consistently shown to be a risk factor. Children who are overprotected may not get enough chances to develop good coping skills in the peer group. As one adolescent girl put it in a focus group with Greek children,[10] "you see, when overprotected, you can't stand up for yourself when you are left on your own".

However these studies of victim characteristics – primarily by psychologists and from behaviour genetics – may give a rather partial picture. This especially depends upon the definition of bullying (see Table 1.1 in Chapter 1). The Dankmeijer definition includes the phrase "when it is difficult to defend themselves due to individual, social or cultural reasons". Individual reasons are those cited previously – if you have low self-esteem it may be more difficult to defend yourself. But social or cultural reasons make explicit that we can also have what is called *bias bullying* or *prejudice-based bullying*. Here someone is at risk of being a victim, not necessarily because of any individual characteristics, but simply by virtue of being in a different group that has a less powerful position (in the school, community or wider society).

In the UK, the Equality and Human Rights Commission lists nine *Protected Characteristics* for which discrimination should not occur. One of these (marriage and civil partnership) will not apply to school-aged children, and another (pregnancy and maternity) only rarely. But the other seven are relevant: age, sex, sexual orientation, gender reassignment, race, religion or belief and disability.

The importance of these will vary by context; for example, racial bullying would not have been much of an issue in Norway or Sweden in the 1970s, when Olweus did his early research, as those countries were much more ethnically homogeneous then than they are now. By contrast, currently many schools in European countries have a quite mixed ethnic composition; the focus group quotes in Chapter 2 illustrated this in an English school which had many Muslim pupils.

The Anti-Bullying Alliance in the UK defines sexual bullying as any bullying behaviour with a sexual element.[11] This would include sexual harassment, such as sexual taunts and threats, or inappropriate and unwanted physical contact. It would also include bullying related to sexual orientation. This is a prominent risk factor. Being lesbian or gay, bisexual or transgender (LGBT), or even questioning your gender orientation (Q) or being perceived to be different in these ways, has been consistently shown to raise the risk of being bullied. This is most marked for adolescent boys who are, or are suspected of being, gay.

In the UK, the Stonewall organization has been active in campaigning around the issues of homophobic, biphobic and transphobic bullying, and assessing their extent.[12] As one 15 year old commented:

> I've been bullied all my school life, but when I came out as gay five years ago, and then as trans two years ago, the bullying increased. People call me a 'he-she', 'tranny', and other transphobic slurs. People also call me homophobic slurs like 'lezza' and 'fag'.

The sample of 3,713 LGBT pupils in the Stonewall survey may not be fully representative, but 45% reported being bullied because of their sexual orientation (this being 64% for trans pupils). One positive finding from the 2017 report was that the figure of 45% victims was less than in 2012 (at 55%) and 2007 (at 65%).

Disability is another major risk factor for being victimized. Here some particular characteristics of a disabled pupil – having a stammer, being hard of hearing, being clumsy – may make them an easy target for other children who enjoy bullying; but also there is often a general prejudice against those with any disability. A child with a disability, especially when in mainstream education, may have fewer friends and struggle to have high social status in the peer group, thus lessening two known protective factors. Other personal characteristics, such as being overweight for example, would not usually be classed as a disability, but can also increase the risk of being victimized.

WHAT DO WE KNOW ABOUT THE BULLY-VICTIMS?

The bully-victims are those falling into both risk groups – bullies and victims. A lot depends here on what criteria are used in defining these groups. As we saw in Chapter 2, there is a lot of variation in quantitative studies (whether questionnaire based or nomination based) on prevalence rates, depending on such criteria. If we use very lenient or inclusive criteria (have you ever bullied others? have you ever been bullied?), then we will get a large proportion of bullies, a large proportion of victims and hence a generous proportion of bully-victims. I would be one myself on these criteria! But suppose we take more usual, somewhat stricter criteria (such as being involved several times in the last school term). Then we get a smaller proportion of bullies, a smaller proportion of victims, and correspondingly a much smaller proportion of bully-victims, which then shrinks dramatically, often to around 1% or 2%.

This small minority of children may share many of the less desirable characteristics of which both the bullies and victims are liable to. They may be both aggressive or disruptive, but also lacking in social skills, having low self-esteem and being unpopular in the peer group. The behaviour genetic study referred to earlier found quite high heritability of the bully-victim status or linkage, and suggested it might be due to a common factor of *emotional dysregulation*, meaning difficulty in managing one's emotions appropriately in different situations. Emotion dysregulation has been found to be highly heritable. Emotion dysregulation might also have environmental causes. A finding from a number of family studies is that bully-victims are especially likely to experience neglect or abuse in the family environment.[13] If parents, who are supposed to love you, sometimes behave neglectfully or abusively, then for the child growing up in this environment, managing emotions and generally managing relationships well is liklely to be challenging.

WHAT DO WE KNOW ABOUT DEFENDERS AND BYSTANDERS?

The majority of children and young people are not involved regularly in bullying (as either bully or victim). Furthermore, most studies of attitudes to bullying suggest that, while some bullies are seen as powerful, and while some victims are unpopular, nevertheless, bullying is largely disliked. But it makes a big difference to the bullies, and the victims, depending on whether this rather 'silent majority' actually does something to help the victims (defenders) or play no active part and thus tacitly condone the bullying (bystanders).

It might be thought that affective empathy would be a distinguishing characteristic for defenders. To some extent this is the case – defenders do tend to score high on this – but other factors are also very important. These are self-efficacy in defending (do they feel confident they know what to do and can do it), and high social status (being liked a lot) in the peer group. This makes sense. To defend a victim, the potential defender needs to feel confident that he or she has the skills to do so – for example, how to tell the bullies that he or she will help the victim, without antagonizing them unnecessarily. Also, there is going to be a risk that the bullies turn on the defender, but this is less likely if the defender is popular, and perhaps has friends to call on for help if need be.

AGE AND GENDER

Age and gender are both factors in the risk of being involved in bullying. So far as age is concerned, the main finding is that victim rates generally decline with age, while bully perpetration rates do not (they stay rather steady). It is also found that physical bullying tends to decline with age, but more subtle, indirect or relational forms increase through childhood and adolescence.

Why do victim rates decline with age? There seem to be several reasons. One is that older children have a better understanding of what bullying means and are less likely than younger ones to say they have been bullied when they have just been involved in a fight, for example. Of course this would mean the age decline is not real (to an objective outside observer). But probably there is some real decline, due to many children developing more effective coping skills when they are occasionally teased or attacked. It is thought that children who enjoy bullying look for easy targets – the more vulnerable children. There are probably fewer victims in older age groups, but in some respects, those are victims then will be more serious victims, as they have not managed to learn to cope effectively. In addition, within a school, older children will be relatively bigger and stronger, and so less likely to be bullied – it is unusual to be bullied by children from younger year groups. Several studies have found that – despite the general age decline – there can be a spike in victim rates at school transitions, when the new intakes find themselves the youngest, often in partly unfamiliar peer groups amongst whom status needs to be re-established.

Gender differences are interesting as they may be changing. They depend a lot upon the type of bullying. Boys are more often the perpetrators of bullying, and this is most marked for physical bullying. This is not surprising, as boys tend to be physically stronger than girls. Also physical strength is valued more in boys' peer groups, so it can be quite effective for a male bully to physically attack and humiliate a male victim, in terms of peer group status. There is less gender difference in terms of verbal bullying, and for relational bullying, such as spreading nasty rumours, some studies find girls more likely to be perpetrators. Reputation (for example for being trustworthy, or not sexually promiscuous) is more important in girls' peer groups, so girl bullies may prefer these kinds of methods. This is also true for cyberbullying, where much of the bullying is on social networking sites and involves attacks or slurs on reputation. Girls tend to be more involved in perpetrating in this way. Online gaming however attracts boys more and they are more likely to be involved in cyberbullying in such contexts.

Overall, boys are also more likely to be victims, but in terms of effects sizes, the gender difference here is much smaller. It is found rather consistently for being a victim of traditional bullying. However, it may be reversed for being a victim of cyberbullying, at least in some surveys. Finally, most studies find girls to more often be defenders. An issue with peer support schemes (discussed in Chapter 6) is that more girls more typically volunteer for peer supporter roles than do boys. Girls tend to be more empathic, which may explain this; though as noted earlier, empathy alone is not enough to be an effective defender.

SCHOOL FACTORS

Schools, even in a similar neighbourhood, can vary a lot in levels of bullying. Individual classes in a school can be important, both in terms of attitudes in the class and whether the class or homeroom teacher is concerned about bullying and is seen to take effective action when it occurs. But the school as a whole can be important too. This is shown by the success of school-wide interventions to reduce bullying, discussed in Chapter 6 – they are not completely successful, to be sure, but they can have an appreciable impact. What appears to be important here is that there is a warm and supportive school climate, and relationships between and among pupils and teachers are respectful. In the US, Dewey Cornell and colleagues have argued for the importance of what they call an authoritative school climate.[14] They consider that a safe and effective school will be both structured, and supportive. Structure comes from high disciplinary and academic expectations for students; teachers and other school staff enforce discipline in a strict but fair manner. Supportiveness comes from responsiveness in teacher-student relationships, with teachers and other school staff interacting with students in a respectful, caring and helpful manner.

SOCIETAL FACTORS

As we saw in Chapter 2, countries vary in the prevalence of bullying, even if there is not a very good agreement amongst the various cross-national surveys as to which countries do best or worst. We are now at the macrosystem level in the ecological model (Figure 3.1).

The possible explanations for country differences are only beginning to be explored. One useful framework for examining this was put forward by the EU Kids online project (see Chapter 2). Their model includes the inner circles of the ecological model (individual, parents/family, peers, school), but has a particularly interesting focus on the outer or macrosystem level, which they call 'country as unit of analysis'. Here there are five aspects.

Cultural values: refers to aspects such as prevalent attitudes and ways of thinking in a society. One well-known dimension here is individualism vs. collectivism. Individualism refers to societies with loose ties, where individuals are expected to look after themselves and immediate family; whereas in collectivism, people are integrated from birth onward into strong, cohesive in-groups which protect them in exchange for loyalty to the group. It has been hypothesized that this might affect levels of bullying (perhaps less in collectivist societies, though this is unproven), and types of bullying (perhaps less physical and more relational in collectivist societies, given the importance of group belonging in the latter). Another relevant dimension is power distance. This refers to the extent to which less powerful members (e.g. in a school) expect and accept that power is distributed unequally. There is more respect for older persons. This may actually affect what is considered as bullying, as compared to accepted normative behaviour. A third interesting dimension is masculinity-femininity. A more masculine society is one where gender roles are distinct (less overlapping): men are more assertive, tough and focussed on material success, while women are more modest and tender. This clearly might have implications for gender differences and for sexual harassment. These suggestions still need further study.

Education system: refers to how schooling is organized. This would include aspects such as ages of school transitions, class groupings, school and class size, structure of school day, break times and supervision, and grade retention. As one example, grade retention (where pupils have to repeat a year due to poor performance) has been associated with higher bullying levels; pupils held back in this way may well be resentful, plus they are now in a class with mainly younger and thus more vulnerable pupils.

Technological infrastructure: in the EU Kids online study, referred mainly to penetration of mobile phones, smart phones and the internet. This obviously affects opportunities for cyberbullying. However other mass media, such as television, movies and computer games, vary between countries, especially for example in the levels of violence permitted. Although there is some controversy about the size of the effect, most studies suggest that exposure to violent media is associated with greater aggression and, in some studies, bullying.

Regulatory framework: refers to what is being done at the societal level to reduce bullying. This would include laws against bullying;

requirements for schools to have anti-bullying policies, or to record bullying incidents and anti-bullying resources and initiatives at a national level. Some studies in the US have suggested an impact of introducing legislation against school bullying (see Chapter 6); in Finland the KiVA anti-bullying initiative appears to be reducing bullying levels over the last decade (see Chapter 7).

Socio-economic stratification: refers primarily to how wealthy a country is and also to levels of income inequality. Related aspects such as health and life expectancy may also be examined. A few studies have concluded that country wealth, measured for example by GDP, is a negative predictor of bully or victim rates (the rates are less in more wealthy countries); this might be because poorer countries can invest less in anti-bullying training and resources, for example. But also income inequality, measured for example by the Gini coefficient, has been found to have a strong association. Perhaps feelings of resentment and distrust are greater in societies with high income inequality, such that violent and bullying behaviours are seen as more acceptable.

4

DOES IT MATTER IF BULLYING HAPPENS IN SCHOOL, AND WHAT ARE THE EFFECTS AND CONSEQUENCES OF BULLYING?

Attitudes to bullying have changed in recent decades. Not so long ago, it was rather common to hear that bullying was a natural part of growing up, something you should just learn to cope with. Although less common now, these views have not gone away. In fact, in 2009, Helene Guldberg, from the Open University in England, stirred up controversy about this. In an article titled "Sorry, but it can be GOOD for children to be bullied",[1] she said that

> Stamping out bullying, saying no to bullying, zero tolerance on bullying . . . are sentiments intended to protect pupils from every unpleasant playground experience, from name-calling to physical fights, and reflect the modern obsession with shielding children from every conceivable danger. . . . But in reality they are robbing them of the opportunity to learn some of life's most valuable lessons. . . . It is not to ignore the tragic stories of the real victims of bullying, but precisely because of them that I feel we must stop the anti-bullying bandwagon from muddying the waters. . . . Today's obsession with the long-term effects of bullying means children are growing up without the social skills or toughness to exist and compete in the adult world. To me, that seems far more damaging to their development and their relationships with each other than any fight or insult could ever be.

The idea that bullying toughens you up for real life is still held quite strongly by some people, and it deserves to be considered seriously. I think there is a kernel of truth in Guldberg's argument. In particular, we possibly worry too much about the odd fight or insult between equals. Clearly there are skills to develop in coping with provocations, and it is desirable to develop such skills.

The flaw in the argument is that bullying is not between equals. As almost all definitions of bullying make clear (Table 1.1), bullying involves an imbalance of power. It specifically does not include the odd fight or quarrel between reasonably equally matched peers. It is difficult for the victim to defend himself or herself. This difficulty may stem from lack of confidence, lack of physical strength, lack of friends to support them being outnumbered or it may be related to prejudice, either because of gender, gender orientation, race/ethnicity, faith or disability. For victims of bullying, the damage to their development can in some cases be profound and long lasting. This was suggested by the two case studies at the start of this book. But it is also supported by a substantial body of research, which we will look at in the second half of the chapter. But first, can children and young people cope on their own with being bullied? What strategies do they actually use, and what is likely to work best?

COPING ON YOUR OWN

Suppose someone pushes you, or insults you, or spreads a nasty story about you. This might be a one-off, or it might be the start of a repeated pattern. In fact, how you react, or cope, with this provocation may well influence how likely this is to continue, and thus become bullying. After all, perpetrators of bullying are often looking for soft targets, who react in ways which are rewarding for them and do not effectively challenge their status.

It may be that you find a way to cope with this effectively. If you are confident, and perhaps have good friends with you, then you can be assertive, challenging what they are doing, saying how you do not like it and if it does not stop you are going to tell adults about it. Or you might fight back. Fighting back is not encouraged by teachers, but I have heard several people tell me how fighting back did stop it and they were not bothered any more. It can work in some cases.

But suppose you are not very confident, not very physically strong or do not have many (or any) good friends who will defend you. Attempts to be assertive may be difficult and could backfire if not done confidently. Fighting back could be a dangerous option as well, and there is the danger of making things worse than before. What strategy would you use? When pupils are asked themselves, some common ones are internalizing strategies (such as feeling upset, crying), distancing (ignoring it, avoiding the bullies), externalizing strategies (such as fighting back), problem-solving (changing one's behaviour, staying with friends) or seeking help or support. There are common gender differences found here, with girls more often asking friends or adults for help, whereas boys more often report fighting back.

The usual advice given in anti-bullying resources and websites is to tell an adult, such as a teacher or parent. The extent to which this is done, and who is told, seems to vary greatly in different contexts. A consistent finding is that rates of telling a teacher are less in older pupils, as well as in boys. Older boys seem to often feel it is a sign of weakness to seek help in this way.

There is evidence that seeking support can be a good strategy. In one study of pupils aged 13–16 years in English schools,[2] the five most frequent coping strategies were talking to someone, followed by ignoring it, sticking up for yourself, avoiding the bullies and making more/different friends. The researchers looked at whether the strategy victims used predicted whether they were still a victim 2 years later. Those who had stopped being victims had more often had talked to someone about it (67%), compared to those who had stayed victims (46%).

Another study, in Sweden,[3] used a quite different method, namely retrospective reports, that also suggested that seeking support was a good strategy. The researchers asked 18-year old college students who had been bullied during their school career what had made the bullying stop (if it did). The most frequent reply was support from school personnel (25%). This was followed by the transition to a new school level (23%), a change of coping strategies (20%), support from parents, change of appearance or way of being (each 12%) and change of school or class, or making new friends (each 11%). In this sample, fighting back did not appear as one of the ways these students thought had been successful.

The success of telling teachers will depend on the school context and clearly needs a consistent and effective response from teaching staff. Interestingly, a study comparing what pupils thought was best to do in England and Japan[4] found that most pupils in England suggested that the victim should seek help from others (teachers, parents and friends), whereas fewer Japanese pupils suggested this. Japanese pupils seemed reluctant to seek help from others; instead they appeared to think taking direct action against bullies was a more useful coping strategy. Many pupils in Japan thought that telling teachers and/or parents could make the situation even worse, and were only likely to tell their friends. These differences may be because a culture of seeking help has been encouraged for some 25 years in English schools, following the national anti-bullying pack *Don't Suffer in Silence*, first published in 1994. Such a national approach has not been emphasized so much in Japan (see Chapter 6).

Coping with cyberbullying: coping with being a victim of cyberbullying may require some partly different strategies. One rather distinctive recommendation is to keep records such as screenshots of any derogatory material as possible evidence in future. Pupils may also try blocking messages, or changing email addresses or mobile phone numbers, but these are probably more short-term solutions. Just as for traditional victimization, problem-solving strategies and seeking help and support may be better approaches. But the equivalent of fighting back may make things worse. One study in the US obtained qualitative interview data on coping strategies from 12 to 14 year olds.[5] An example of a problem-solving strategy was "I contacted and confronted the person. I asked her to delete the mean comments" (13-year-old girl); and of help seeking, "I talked to my friends and family, and asked if they could help me" (13-year-old girl). An ignoring strategy, which can sometimes work, was illustrated by a 13-year-old boy: "I ignored the person, avoided him at school, and just dropped it". More problematic, as likely to continue and indeed aggravate the situation, could be aggressive retaliation. An example of this came from a 14-year-old boy: "I was so angry that I went to a forum and started trolling everyone on it. Then I sent a message to his friends and said that he was talking about them". This suggests a cyberbully/victim pattern of behaviour.

A study in Portugal,[6] with mainly 11–16 year olds, examined whom cyber victims turned to for support. The findings, shown in Table 4.1, are that friends were told most often, followed by parents, with teachers the least likely to be told. This low likelihood of telling teachers is a typical pattern for cyber victims especially. Several studies have found that telling a teacher (compared to telling a friend, parent or sibling) is considerably less frequent for cyber victims compared to traditional victims. It may be that many teachers are not seen by pupils as sufficiently prepared to tackle cyberbullying, whereas ways of dealing with traditional bullying have improved over the last decade or so (Chapter 6). This may change, as schools gain a new generation of younger teachers more familiar with the internet and social networking. The school can help too by fostering a climate of trust and responsibility (see Chapter 5). In fact, in the Portuguese study, telling teachers was more likely amongst those cyber victims who had a positive perception of school climate.

Another typical finding, evident in Table 4.1, is that whether it is friends, parents or teachers, girls are more likely to seek support than

Table 4.1 Likelihood of Portuguese cyber victims telling friends, parents and teachers about it (mean responses: 1 = did not tell, 2 = did tell)

	Male victims	Female victims	Overall
Friends	1.24	1.42	1.37
Parents	1.15	1.33	1.28
Teachers	1.04	1.13	1.10

boys. It is worrying that boys are relatively reluctant to seek help, as it is generally found to be a helpful strategy. This was mentioned previously for traditional victimization, and has also been found for cyber victimization. For example, a longitudinal study in 12 Swiss schools[7] examined depression and coping strategies in 13 year olds, in relation to both traditional and cyber victimization. Over time, support seeking was associated with reduced depression.

THE EFFECTS OF BEING INVOLVED IN BULLYING

There are well-established consequences of being a victim of bullying. These can be short-term (immediate, or at least while still at school) and long-term (persisting into adult life). There are also consequences for perpetrating bullying and for the bully-victims, who need to be considered separately. A review[8] of all three roles (victim, bully, bully-victim) concluded that "childhood bullying has serious effects on health, resulting in substantial costs for individuals, their families and society at large", and that "bullying by peers has been mostly ignored by health professionals but should be considered as a significant risk factor and safeguarding issue". In fact the negative impact of long-term victimization appears comparable to the effects of being put into care as a child!

THE EFFECTS OF BEING VICTIMIZED: SHORT-TERM

Anyone who has experienced being bullied knows that it can lead to anxiety and depression, feelings of loneliness and lack of self-worth or self-esteem. Being victimized can be a risk factor for self-harm, suicidal attempts and actual suicide. And there are plenty of studies making such associations. However there is a problem in interpretation here. As we saw in Chapter 3, children who are lonely or lack confidence and self-esteem are more at risk of being bullied. So what is the causal relationship here – is it that loneliness leads to being bullied (for example), or that being bullied leads to loneliness?

The bottom line here is that, first, the causal direction probably goes both ways; but that, second, there is very good evidence that being a victim does directly contribute to these kinds of negative outcomes. A careful review of the evidence[9] drew on two main sources: longitudinal studies and discordant monozygotic (MZ – identical) twin studies.

Longitudinal studies are carried out over a time period, often of a few years. Typically, measurements might be made of whether someone was victimized (or how often) and also of their self-esteem, friendships, depression or mental health, or other measures thought to be relevant. Take self-esteem as an example here. The researcher can assess whether being or becoming a victim leads to lower self-esteem at a later time, or whether low self-esteem at an earlier time predicts an increase in victimization later. Sometimes measurements are just taken at two time points, but the analyses and conclusions are more convincing if there are three or more time points to compare.

The evidence from a number of longitudinal studies shows that, while there is evidence for both directions of effect (suggesting a 'vicious circle' of influence), there is clearly evidence that being victimized is associated with increases in mental health symptoms such as depression, as well as other possible psychotic symptoms such as sleep disturbance, difficulties in concentration or suicidal thoughts. These studies typically also control for some confounders. A confounder is a measure, such as gender or IQ or socioeconomic status, that could influence or even explain the findings (for example, low intelligence might be responsible for both low self-esteem and risk of victimization). These obvious confounders are often controlled for by statistical analyses that show that they are not responsible (or not substantially responsible) for the links found. But, of course, there might be other confounders that were not thought of or not examined.

The discordant MZ twin design is a way around this difficulty. MZ, or monozygotic, twins are identical twins – they have the same genetic inheritance. However they might be discordant – they might differ from each other – on some environmentally influenced characteristic. As applied here, researchers would assess MZ twins who are discordant for victim status. Of the twins, one has been bullied at school, the other not; this might result, for example, from them being in different classes at school, or having different friends. The twins can then be compared on a measure of interest such as self-esteem. The twins are not only genetically identical, but come from the same family environment. Thus genetic and also many (although not all) environmental influences are in common, and it is likely that any differences found in self-esteem are due to the experience of being a victim. Such studies have found that victimized twins have more emotional problems, such as social anxiety, and are more likely to self-harm, than their non-victimized co-twin.

Furthermore, what is called a *dose-response relationship* is very often found. This means that a larger 'dose' or experience of victimization is associated with worse outcomes. Here, the 'dose' might be how frequent the experience is, how severe the incidents were, how long they went on for and how many types of bullying were experienced (this latter is considered further later). Finally, negative outcomes generally lessen if the victimization eases off or stops. There is very strong evidence then that experiences of being a victim can indeed cause negative outcomes, notably mental health difficulties such as depression.

However not all children are affected the same way – some are strongly affected, some appear more resilient. In other words, the effects of victimization can be moderated by other factors. Some factors that might help a child be resilient are the warmth and supportiveness of the family environment, support from friends and being good at some activity (such as a sport or hobby) that boosts their self-esteem. Conversely, some factors that might exacerbate effects of victimization are having a difficult or even abusive family environment, having few or no good friends or not having some activity you can feel confident about.

These moderating factors are very important when we consider the risk of suicidal thoughts, or of suicide. Some studies have found that victimized children – and especially the bully-victims – are at greater risk of self-harm, suicidal ideation and even actual suicide. Cases of suicides, apparently due to bullying, can be picked up by the media; they can have a dramatic impact on public awareness of the consequences of bullying (as mentioned in Chapter 1). The term *bullicide* has been coined for this, and *cyberbullicide* when cyberbullying has been involved.

A number of such cases get reported every year. For example, in the US, NBC News reported how a 12-year-old girl had taken her own life after allegedly being bullied by her classmates. According the family's lawyer, her life "tragically ended when her own classmates used this cellphone to drive her into this tragedy. . . . For months there were texts, Snapchat and Instagram – she was told she was a loser, she had no friends. She was even told, "why don't you kill yourself". Her mother commented, "It got to the point where she didn't want to go to school. She had chronic headaches, stomach aches . . . Her grades plummeted". Her family felt the school had done little to protect her and sued the school district for negligence.[10]

It has been pointed out that other factors, such as pre-existing depression, or family or other relationship difficulties, can interact with the experience of being a victim to greatly increase the risk of suicide. There can be multiple causes when this happens. Nonetheless, it can be clear from the circumstances, and sometimes from a suicide note left by the victim, that the continued experiences of being bullied have been a major factor in such tragic circumstances.

EFFECTS OF BEING VICTIMIZED: LONG-TERM

Being a victim of bullying clearly affects someone immediately and in the short-term – the weeks and maybe months following. But are there long-term effects, even perhaps after leaving school and after the bullying has stopped? Case studies, as illustrated by the quotes from the Webster's book, and from the 36-year-old woman who had a stammer at school, suggest that there can indeed be effects still present many years later.

This has been confirmed by research on larger samples. It has been found that victims of bullying at school are more likely to have anxiety disorders and mental health problems, such as being depressed, later in life. One group of researchers reviewed 28 longitudinal studies.[11] The mean follow-up period was 7 years, so mostly measures were obtained with young adults. The probability of being depressed was much higher if they had been bullied at school. On average, the odds ratio was 1.99. This means that if you had been bullied at school, you were almost twice as likely to be depressed than if you had not been bullied at school. As mentioned before, there is the same possibility of other, confounding factors that might explain the association. But after controlling for up to 20 major childhood risk factors, the odds ratio was still 1.74.

Why might being victimized at school have such long-term effects? Mental health issues such as low self-esteem and depression do tend to persist, and we saw earlier that there is evidence for a vicious cycle, with (for example) depression causing someone to be more vulnerable to victimization, and then being a victim making the depression worse. Being victimized does not necessarily stop after leaving school (Chapter 7), so it may take some clear life changes or some therapeutic intervention to break this.

Research has also suggested a biological mechanism which may play a part in this. If we are stressed (as for example by someone attacking or trying to bully us), the body mobilizes for a response. Stress hormones, such as adrenaline and cortisol, alert the body to take action. Adrenaline is released quickly, cortisol more slowly but staying for longer. Cortisol can be measured from saliva, and several research studies have been carried out on cortisol levels in victims of bullying. Typically, their cortisol responses are low to a stressor compared to non-victimized controls. This might seem counter-intuitive; but the explanation is probably that this is an adaptive response. Getting worked up (heart beating fast) and vigilant if attacked can be adaptive in the short-term, but it is costly energetically and puts a strain on bodily resources. If you are being bullied frequently, it just may not be feasible for your body to keep responding in this energetic way. So the response of the victim becomes muted; but this too has a cost, of course, as he or she is less likely to respond effectively, and is more likely to feel helpless and thus depressed.

CONSEQUENCES FOR PERPETRATORS OF BULLYING

Depending on the school climate, attitudes of peers and responses to bullying incidents, the perpetrators of bullying may get short-term gains from their actions (Chapter 3). They may get a reputation as a powerful individual; in adolescence they may be attractive to the opposite sex as a potential dating partner. They may be able to extract money or other material goods from a victim. In Japan, a notable case was the suicide of 13-year-old Kiyoteru Okouchi in 1994, who hanged himself from a tree in the family garden. He had been terrorized for three years by a gang of four classmates who extracted the equivalent of more than $10,000 from him. Much of this Kiyoteru stole from his parents. He left a note detailing his guilt and suffering, ending: "I wanted to live longer, but . . .".

In the short term, then, this gang of bullies gained a lot of money. But they were setting out on a path of delinquent and anti-social behaviour, with likely adverse consequences in the medium to longer term. The research shows clearly that there are longer-term correlates, and quite possibly consequences, of bullying others at school. One is a considerably greater risk for later offending and violent behaviour. One meta-analysis review examined findings from 29 longitudinal studies.[12] The mean follow-up period was 6 years. The probability of offending was much higher for children who were bullies at school, with a mean odds ratio of 2.64, so they were over two-and-a-half times more likely to be offenders than those who had not bullied others at school. After adjusting for a range of other factors, the odds ratio was still 1.89.

CONSEQUENCES FOR BULLY-VICTIMS

The bully-victims generally suffer the adverse effects of victims, but in addition tend to be impulsive and have poor regulation of emotions. One study (using HBSC data, see Chapter 1) compared correlates of victim, bully and bully-victim roles, compared to non-involved pupils, for 11–15 year olds across 25 countries.[13] The results were fairly consistent. Victims scored lowest on emotional adjustment and relationships with classmates; bullies scored low on school adjustment, and high on alcohol use. The bully-victims scored poorly in all these aspects. In fact they generally have the poorest outcomes (compared to 'pure' victims or bullies) on measures of mental health, social relationships and long-term outcomes such as educational attainment.

EFFECTS ON EDUCATIONAL ATTAINMENT

Findings on educational attainment are mixed. Sometimes a young person may be bullied because he or she is seen as a swot, or as a teacher's pet. This would bring about a positive correlation with educational achievement. On the other hand, the anxiety and stress caused by victimization experiences are likely to lead to school absenteeism and poorer educational attainment. Most studies find a modest negative association between educational attainment and the victim role. The negative association is stronger for bullies, and especially bully-victims, who are often disaffected from school and not so motivated to do well.

In the longer term, some analyses were carried out in the UK using data from the National Child Development Study or NCDS.[14] The NCDS has followed all children born during one week in 1958, initially totaling 17,634. They were followed up at ages 7, 11, 16, 23, 33 and 42 on a variety of measures (and subsequently to 55 after the analyses here were reported). It was possible to get measures of victim involvement at ages 7 and 11, and bully involvement at age 16. These were related to educational attainment (number of O levels; and getting a degree) at ages 23, 33 and 42. The victims of school bullying had lower educational attainment into adulthood (than non-victims), even after controlling for some school and family characteristics. The perpetrators of bullying had even worse educational attainment, doing significantly poorer than that of the victims.

CONSEQUENCES FOR BYSTANDERS AND FOR THE SCHOOL CLIMATE

Those who witness bullying are likely to be affected by it. Of course a lot will depend on how the bullying is dealt with and if there are seen to be consequences; but, in any event, it is likely to be upsetting. One study[15] was made of about 2,000 pupils aged 12–16, from schools in England. Assessments of mental health symptoms, such as somatic complaints and depression, showed that witnesses of bullying scored worse than those who had not witnessed bullying (although not so poorly as victims, or often perpetrators).

TRADITIONAL AND CYBER VICTIMIZATION COMPARED

Besides the frequency, severity and duration of victimization experiences, another factor can be the number of types of bullying that are experienced. Is it worse to be both physically and verbally assaulted? Maybe socially excluded as well? And perhaps also being cyberbullied? Being bullied in various ways is called *polyvictimization*. Studies which have examined this typically find that being bullied in various different ways is worse than just being bullied in one way. This is understandable. If you are unable to defend yourself effectively, either physically, verbally, socially or on the internet, then this could have multiple damaging effects on different areas of one's self-esteem.

Another area where much research has been done is in comparing the relative impact of traditional (offline) and cyber (online) victimization. There are arguments both ways about their relative impact. Being a cyber victim is often perceived as having greater impact, for at least two reasons. One is the wider potential audience – hundreds or thousands of visitors might see a humiliating picture or message on a website, compared to the dozen or so who might see or hear about a playground humiliation. The second is the 24/7 nature of cyberbullying – there is no respite, unlike the evenings, weekends and holidays when there is a respite from traditional bullying. On the other hand, some children (more often boys) seem able to minimize the impact of cyberbullying because they perceive it as, in a sense, not real – you are not actually physically hurt or damaged. Relative impact may vary by gender, and the actual types within traditional or cyberbullying, but the empirical evidence so far is that being a cyber victim has impacts just as severe, and sometimes more so, than traditional bullying; while those who experience both traditional and cyberbullying are the worst affected.

5

WHAT OTHERS CAN DO TO HELP

The previous chapter discussed what children who are victims of bullying may do to try and cope with it. This sometimes works, but often does not, as the victim is often being bullied by any number of more powerful other children and cannot easily defend himself or herself. What can others do to help? This chapter will first consider what parents can do – how they can find out about bullying and what actions they can take. Then, this chapter will consider what friends and peers can do, perhaps by defending the victim, and especially the role of peer support systems in schools. Preventative work by the school, such as embedding social and e-safety skills in the curriculum, and working on playground supervision and design, will then be considered.

PARENTS AND FAMILIES

Parents have an important role to play in at least three ways. First, they can provide a happy, secure environment for their child(ren). Second, they can be alert to signs of involvement in bullying and be supportive if their child tells them about it. Third, they can liaise constructively with the school and any anti-bullying program the school may be using.

There are plenty of manuals on parenting, and there is not a universal agreement on the best way to parent – for example on how strict to be about rules in the house. But there is quite strong agreement in the research literature that providing a warm and secure environment for children will help them be more confident and resilient. In such families there is a clear framework of expectations, coupled with the children knowing that ultimately they are loved by the parents. This is sometimes called an *authoritative* parenting style, and usually emerges as the best, although there are some cultural differences in how this is expressed. As we saw in Chapter 3, children who bully others are more likely to come from homes where there is conflict within the family, and victims may come from over-protective families.

As we saw in Chapter 4, many victims of bullying suffer in silence. They may not tell anyone about it. Parents can be alert to signs of their children being bullied: they may seem less happy without any obvious reason, less willing or enthusiastic to go to school, not seeing, visiting or bringing back friends so often, not sleeping well, getting unexpectedly poor grades at school or showing signs of low self-esteem, depression or self-harm. Gentle discussion about the reasons for this may elicit being bullied as a factor. In such circumstances, parents can provide considerable support.

They can point out that, in fact, many children get bullied, including some famous ones (see for example Jessica Ennis-Hill's account in her book *Unbelievable*, 2012).[1] They can suggest practical steps to take – useful coping strategies, such as staying with friends and, where possible, being assertive; keeping a record of incidents or screenshots of cyberbullying; and, with the aid of the school anti-bullying policy, consulting with the class teacher and if necessary the head teacher, or school governors. Many schools have specific staff to liaise with parents (home–school workers; parent support advisors).

Parents have a particular role in cyberbullying as regards knowing about and advising on their child's internet use. The evidence suggests that this is best done by concerned involvement but without being overly restrictive. Parents also may become aware that their child is a bullying perpetrator, or even a bystander; here they can help by discussing the harm that bullying can cause, the feelings and hurt of victims and the moral imperative to stop bullying or to defend victims so far as is feasible. Many anti-bullying programs also involve parents (Chapter 7), so here too parents have a role to play in supporting the schools' actions.

The general family environment matters too when we consider the part siblings may have in either supporting a bullied child, or possibly exacerbating the situation. Potentially a sibling can be a source of support, either directly if they are in the same school, or else by listening and providing reassurance in the home environment. However sometimes siblings themselves may be in a bullying relationship within the family. A consistent finding is that sibling bullying is associated with school bullying – being a victim (or bully) in one context makes it rather more likely that you will be a victim (or bully) in the other. Here again parents have an important part to play in fostering a constructive rather than conflictual environment for all children in the family.

PEERS IN THE SCHOOL AND PEER-SUPPORT SCHEMES

Just as siblings might (or might not) have a supportive role in the family, so peers might (or might not) have a supportive role at school. As discussed in Chapter 2, having friends, especially loyal friends who stand by you, and especially friends with some status in the peer group, are significant protective factors against being bullied. However, not all children have such friends. Peer support schemes provide a way of harnessing the goodwill of the majority of pupils in the school, to help victims or potential victims of bullying.

Peer support uses the experience, knowledge and skills of pupils in a planned and structured way. It can be used for a variety of purposes, but a common one is to reduce bullying and provide support for victims. Many schools now use some kind of peer-support system, of which there is a considerable variety. Important aspects are the selection of peer supporters, training and monitoring, the facilities provided by the school and the type of scheme used.

Selection: peer supporters may volunteer for the role or be selected either by school staff or by student nomination. There are pros and cons to each method. Volunteers will likely be enthusiastic and committed to the role, but may not necessarily have high status in the peer group. Those nominated by pupils may have status, but not be so committed. Either way, it is also important to get a gender balance; girls tend to volunteer for peer-supported roles more than boys, but boys are in just as much need of peer support. Teacher nomination, or some gender-quota arrangement, can help ensure such a balance.

Training and monitoring: peer supporters need training, both in implementing the scheme(s) chosen, but also in matters such as basic counselling skills, confidentiality and ethics. They need to know what is within their remit, and when they need to get help from an adult or refer on the situation encountered. Training can be provided by an outside agency, or by a teacher who has already been trained. Usually a trained teacher in the school will be responsible for overseeing the peer-support scheme, and they should arrange regular debriefing sessions to discuss how things are going with the peer support scheme, and any problems encountered. It is also desirable to try and assess the impact that the scheme might be having.

Facilities provided by the school: if a peer-support scheme is to work well, it needs support from the senior management of the school. Besides releasing some time for the teacher who is coordinating the peer-support system, there needs to be provision for advertising the scheme. Peer supporters might be identified by badges, or via a special notice board with their photographs and/or special introductory assemblies. Also there must be a way for pupils who want to use the service to make contact with the peer supporters. There are various ways to contact peer supporters. Primary schools might have a bench in the playground where children can go if they are feeling sad or have no one to play with, and a peer supporter will then go to talk to them. In secondary schools, there is more commonly a confidential area, such as a private room, manned by peer supporters at designated times, such as lunch breaks, where pupils can go to seek help.

Alternatively, contact can be made through a bully box (where messages can be posted) or via the school intranet.

The type of scheme used: here there is a huge variety. In primary schools, buddies and befrienders generally look out for pupils at break times who are upset or lonely. Playleaders or Playground pals lead structured games activities. In the secondary sector, peer supporters, usually from older year groups, can be used at transition for incoming pupils. They can also provide one-to-one mentoring for bullied students in a designated room or at a lunchtime club. Schemes include buddy schemes, peer mentoring, peer listening/counselling and peer mediation.

Circle time/circles of friends/circles of support/supportive friends: these circles could involve a whole class of pupils, or selected pupils. The teacher helps pupils discuss feelings, develop flexible and creative methods to form positive relationships with peers and develop empathic skills and creativity. This can help pupils feel less isolated in the knowledge that some peers would help if they were in difficulties. These circle times can be important for restorative approaches (see Chapter 6).

Befriending: befriending or buddy schemes offer support and friendship from peer supporters to pupils who may be lonely or lacking friends at the time, or perhaps because they are new to the school. Some schemes are based on playground buddies, usually identifiable by special caps/clothing, who help a lonely or bullied child during break times or lunchtimes, when they can feel vulnerable. Other schemes focus on organizing playground games, or on running lunchtime clubs. These can be open to all, but offer companionship to lonely pupils and a way for them to join in. Befrienders can be the same age or older than their target group. In the secondary sector, buddy schemes can be used at transitions to help the incoming pupils adjust to a new school; they may attend registration in some form or tutor for a time in the first term, with their attendance gradually reducing over the year as the new pupils grow in confidence.

Peer mentoring: peer mentoring schemes aim for a supportive relationship between two pupils, combining practical advice and encouragement. They are especially used for supporting a pupil at challenging times (e.g. joining a new school, bereavement or bullying). In secondary schools, older pupil mentors can help train younger ones. Mentoring is a relatively challenging role, so good staff supervision and support is especially important.

Peer mediation: peer mediation is a problem-solving process. It encourages pupils to define the problem, identify and agree on key issues, discuss and brainstorm possible options, negotiate a plan of action and agreement and follow-up and evaluate outcomes. Pupil mediators are trained in conflict resolution skills and in helping individuals resolve disputes.

General evaluation of peer support schemes

There are mixed findings about the success of peer-support schemes, and one review[2] argued that "it seems from our results that work with peers should not be used". There are certainly some problematic issues around peer-support schemes, and some pitfalls to avoid. As an example of the latter, playground buddy schemes can be helpful but may be underused if users feel exposed or stigmatized. A lonely child who sits at a buddy bus stop waiting for help may be exposed to ridicule. Also, the playground buddies may be teased about special badges or clothes; in one school, they wore yellow caps and were consequently teased as being 'banana-heads'. These kinds of difficulties can be avoided by having discrete facilities (such as a private room for pupils to go to) or running more inclusive activities such as lunchtime clubs. Another danger is that, perhaps through inadequate advertising, or opportunities for contact, a scheme is underused, and peer supporters feel demotivated.

In another review,[3] it was argued that peer-support schemes could reduce bullying in three main ways: first, through a general improvement in the school environment; second, through helping individual pupils who use the scheme to stop being victimized and, third, by reducing general rates of bullying throughout the school. There appears to be evidence for the first; schools that run well-managed peer support schemes are seen as being more caring and concerned about pupil well-being, and the schemes are known and supported by pupils and staff. In addition, there is good evidence that the peer supporters themselves generally benefit from the experience; they have gained useful skills in training and, provided the scheme is used effectively, they feel they are doing something useful to help others. As regards the second aim of helping victims, there is certainly evidence for this from individual cases; some pupils who use peer support schemes for reasons of being bullied, do say that it has helped them. As regards the third aim of generally reducing bullying, many relevant studies did not report significant changes in general levels of bullying behaviour as a result of implementing a peer-support scheme.

However, peer support schemes are developing, schools are learning from past experience and new methods are evolving. The KiVa project (see Chapter 7) uses peer support successfully. Some work in Italy[4] has provided an example where a web-based project called *Noncadiamointrappola* (Let's not fall into a trap), or *NoTrap!* for short, has had such success. Here, students at high schools developed a website to promote peer-to-peer content against bullying and cyberbullying, and an evaluation found that cyberbullying others decreased significantly (especially for boys), compared to schools not in the program. In a follow-up study, which involved the teachers and bystanders more, a Facebook page was integrated with the web forum; an evaluation found significant reductions in traditional bully and victim rates, and cyber victim rates, for the experimental group, compared to some increases in the control group.

THE ROLE OF THE SCHOOL

Schools have a vital role to play in having a good anti-bullying policy; using school councils, providing support and training for teachers to deal with bullying effectively; providing pupils with curricula materials or lessons that help prevent bullying and generally encouraging an authoritative school climate where bullying is considered unacceptable.[5]

A whole school anti-bullying policy

In England, it is a legal requirement to determine a school's behaviour policy with a view to encouraging good behaviour and preventing all forms of bullying among pupils. Anti-bullying policies can either be contained in a general behaviour policy or be a separate policy. The policy should be a short document, typically two or three pages, stating what is meant by bullying, some basic information about it and what procedures should be followed should it happen. Most policies contain a definition of bullying, statements about the improvement of school climate and how sanctions relate to the type and severity of the incident. However it is also important to include mentions of forms of bullying such as cyberbullying, homophobic bullying and bullying based on disability or faith. Other important aspects are procedures to follow-up on incidents, and specific preventative measures (such as playground work or peer-support schemes). Not all policies cover these aspects satisfactorily.[6]

Having a good anti-bullying policy does not in itself imply lower rates of school bullying or violence. In fact, there is only very modest evidence for such a direct association. However it does provide a framework for the school's response, involving the whole school community: pupils, teachers, learning mentors, school support staff, governors and parents/carers. It can be important for parents of a bullied child as an initial avenue will be to see if the procedures outlined in the policy are being followed.

School councils

School councils involve students, usually elected representatives, who meet regularly with members of school staff to discuss and decide on policy issues, which can include anti-bullying work. This is the main form of pupil voice in many schools. School councils provide opportunities for student feedback and for schools to listen to them. Specialized forms of school councils include anti-bullying committees, which can be effective in providing feedback about anti-bullying work; if schools use this, it is important to acknowledge and act upon recommendations and feedback, otherwise it becomes 'tokenistic'.

Teachers and teacher training

Teachers are in the front line in terms of implementing school policies on bullying and dealing with incidents if they occur. Studies of both the Olweus Bullying Prevention Program in Norway and the KiVa project in Finland (described in Chapter 7) show that aspects such as teachers awareness of, attention to and communicating about bullying, and the general pupil perception of a homeroom teacher's attitude to bullying, are significant predictors of levels of bullying in the class and the school. These programs, and many others, include some specific training of teachers as part of the package. Teachers should lead by example and model positive relationships, and training can help in this. For example, in one school, staff attitudes had changed during a campaign to address homophobic language; staff who used to laugh, now challenged it, and the campaign was seen as a success.

However, despite the advances in knowledge that we have gained in understanding school bullying and violence, the application of this knowledge to initial teacher training courses is woefully inadequate in many countries. Teachers have to acquire skills on the job or participate in through in-service training should their school invest in this. These are useful, but rather haphazard and piecemeal. This is an area where more effort needs to be made at regional and national levels to help teachers, and trainee teachers, who would often welcome such assistance.

Curricular materials/approaches

Classroom activities can be used to tackle issues associated with bullying, progressively and in an age-, gender- and culturally appropriate way. They can be used to raise awareness, to publicize and discuss the school's anti-bullying policy, and to develop social and emotional skills, empathy and assertiveness in confronting bullying.

Some activities are relatively passive. These might be for example, reading stories or poems about bullying, watching a play about bullying and discussing it afterwards or watching videos. For example, e-safety films used in secondary schools, such as *Let's Fight It Together* (produced by Childnet International, about cyberbullying), and *Exposed* (produced by the Child Exploitation and Online Protection unit, about sexting) have been found to be highly rated by students and staff. However many activities are more active. Pupils can be involved in writing and acting their own play; younger pupils can use puppets and dolls in this way, or debates might be held, or an assembly devised by pupils. A relatively recent development is the use of computer-based games where children can act out roles and see the consequences in a virtual environment (as in KiVa, see Chapter 7).

Used on their own, there is some evidence for positive effects on attitudes and behaviour from such activities. But these are likely to be short term in the case of, say, watching or even designing and acting in one play or performance. These kinds of curricula work do need to be backed up by continuing anti-bullying work and policy.

Co-operative group work: here, pupils work together to solve a common task. This might for example be to design a newspaper. Within a group, pupils have different but complementary roles to complete the task. For this reason, this method is sometimes called the 'jigsaw classroom'. Co-operative group work has the potential to involve and integrate vulnerable, bullied children in the class peer group, since they will have a definite role to play with others and should be supported by them. It has been shown to help in this respect; but the activities can be disrupted by bullying children.

Quality circles: these are problem-solving groups of pupils formed for regular classroom sessions, usually once a week over the course of one school term. Quality circles can be used for a range of topics, including bullying. Pupils in a class might be split into groups of around five or six, and there is a set of procedures to follow concerning group formation, data gathering and presentation of outcomes. In the case of bullying, each group might discuss what the nature of the problem is, how to find out more about it and what can be done about it. They then report back to the class (or possibly the school) at the end of the term. Their suggestions should be listened to and considered; some may be useful, others might be less so or impractical, but this can be conveyed respectfully. Although not widely used, quality circles get good feedback from schools that have used the method. In one UK secondary school, quality circles were found to be an engaging process for pupils, and effective in gathering information on bullying; this was useful to staff in understanding how bullying was changing over time, most especially as regards new forms of cyberbullying. Pupils had their own ideas for dealing with the problem and suggested a range of solutions, some of which were implemented.

Personal, social and health education (PSHE): this can be a main way of delivering anti-bullying work through the curriculum, through regular weekly sessions discussing relationships and healthy and respectful ways of behaving. Through interactive discussion, PSHE can develop pupil awareness of different types of bullying, the consequences of bullying and anti-social behaviour and promote ways of challenging and coping with the effects of bullying. It can provide the opportunity to develop pupils' confidence in coping with bullying by giving and receiving support and developing strategies for conflict resolution. There are various curricula, one example in England having been *Social and Emotional Aspects of Learning* (SEAL), a whole-school approach to developing social and emotional skills, to promote positive behaviour, attendance, learning and well-being. It directly addressed behavioural issues (including bullying) at whole school and individual levels. In the US, and in some other countries, the PATHS program has been used extensively.

Assertiveness training: assertiveness refers to standing up for one's rights, but in a non-violent or non-aggressive way. This can be very useful for all pupils, but especially for those who are bullied or at risk of being bullied. Being able to say, confidently, "I don't like what you are doing. If you go on, then I am going to get help", may not be easy before being practiced in assertiveness training, but can be quite effective. This kind of training teaches a range of specific strategies for dealing with difficult situations, including bullying. Other techniques include 'broken record' (repeatedly saying a response such as "no, I don't want to do that"), and 'fogging' (responding to teasing or insults in a non-committal way, such as "so that's what you think").

Through regular in-class or after school sessions, pupils can talk about their experiences and learn and practice effective responses. This can help victims develop useful strategies, but it does not solve bullying on its own. Assertiveness training can be expensive and time consuming and it does require periodic refresher sessions to be most effective.

E-safety skills: there are specific skills useful to learn for safer internet use, both for pupils and often also for all school personnel and parents or caregivers. It can start with raising awareness of what cyberbullying is, and the harm it can cause. Specific guidelines for safer internet behaviour will be helpful, such as managing privacy settings sensibly, knowing how to report abuse, keeping evidence, getting information on legal rights, knowing helpful websites and sources of support. E-safety skills programs will need updating regularly, since legal issues are likely to change as new precedents are established, and internet service providers are increasingly being held to account concerning how they monitor material, how easy it is to report abuse and how readily action is taken against offensive postings.

WORKING IN THE PLAYGROUND

Traditional bullying in school predominately takes place outside the classroom, sometimes in corridors or school toilets, and often in the school grounds during breaks. An effective playground policy and well-designed play areas can help to reduce rates of bullying.

Playground policy and lunchtime supervisor training: a playground policy includes a strategy for appropriate behaviour in breaks and playtimes, encouraging prosocial playground games and activities and effective liaison between teaching staff and lunchtime supervisors. The lunch-time supervisors have a pivotal role in implementing any playground or school anti-bullying policy, but often receive little or no training for this. Training sessions can provide them with additional skills in organizing games, recognizing bullying behaviours, interviewing pupils and dealing with bullying and conflict situations. One impor-tant aspect is distinguishing bullying from playful fighting. Such training can also raise the self-esteem of lunchtime supervisors and their status in the school community.

Playground design: work on the physical environment of the play-ground can include redesigning it to provide plenty of creative opportunities for pupils during break and lunchtimes, thus reducing boredom and the likelihood of children seeking fun from bullying. It can be useful to set up safe play areas or quiet rooms. Optimizing the playground environment and facilities can be a great opportu-nity for involving pupils. They could be asked to map bullying hot spots; more generally, they could participate in exercises or com-petitions to model different playground designs. It may also be an opportunity to involve parents, who sometimes can supply useful outdoor materials such as old rubber tires, or help in the construc-tion of equipment. Peer support schemes, particularly playleaders and sports mentors, can also be used to provide break time activi-ties and lunchtime clubs, open to anyone but especially helpful for vulnerable pupils.

SCHOOL CLIMATE

At a broader level, the climate of the school can provide a generally supportive environment for pupils in trouble, including those expe-riencing bullying. The authoritative school climate theory[7] posits that two domains of school climate are key to a safe and effective school (Cornell, Shukla & Konold, 2015). The first domain encompasses high disciplinary and academic expectations for students, which has been referred to as the demandingness or *structure* of the school climate. In a structured school, teachers and other school staff members enforce discipline in a strict but fair manner, and they communicate high academic expectations for all students. The second domain concerns the responsiveness or *supportiveness* of teacher–student relationships. In a supportive school, teachers and other school staff members interact with students in a respectful, caring and helpful manner.

6

WHAT IF BULLYING HAPPENS...?

In Chapter 5 we looked at the more *proactive strategies* that a school can take to reduce the likelihood of bullying happening. But it is highly likely that even in the best schools, some bullying incidents will happen. So if a bullying incident does happen in school, what should the school do? The school policy should give some guidance on what actions will be taken. Also, for a serious incident, there may be legal issues to consider. However, in many countries, including the UK, schools do have quite a lot of choice about the way they respond, or in what *reactive strategies* they may use.

The most common reactive strategies are some form of direct sanctions. These involve a negative outcome for the bullying perpetrator and are sometimes referred to as punitive approaches. These can be contrasted with what are often called non-punitive approaches, where the aim is more to change the attitudes and ways of thinking of the child(ren) doing the bullying without invoking any punishment. Yet another strategy, now increasingly used in many schools, is restorative approaches. We will look at the pros and cons of these different approaches, and what evidence there is for their effectiveness.

LEGAL ISSUES

In many countries, bullying *per se* is not a criminal offence, but some severe kinds of bullying may be. For example, in the UK, the Department for Education guidance[1] makes it clear that some types of harassing or threatening behaviour, or communications (e.g. online) which are indecent or grossly offensive and intended to cause distress, may be a criminal office, in which case the school should contact the police. The relevant legislation is spread across several Acts: the Public Order Act (1986) for harassing or threatening behaviour, the Children Act (1989) for safeguarding and the Equality Act (2010) for prejudice-based bullying. For serious cases of cyberbullying, the Malicious Communications Act (1988), the Protection from Harassment Act (1997) and the Communications Act (2003, section 127) can be used, and the Criminal Justice and Courts Act (2015, section 33) for revenge pornography/sexting.

In the US, all 50 states now have some an anti-bullying law to prevent bullying. A couple of studies have given some indication of what impact these might have. One study used data from 25 states at a time when these varied in how strong anti-bullying legislation was. Those states with stronger legislation tended to have lower rates of pupils being bullied, even after some confounding factors were taken account of. Another study in Iowa used a longitudinal design.[2] The researchers compared rates of bullying in 2005, just before an anti-bullying law was introduced, with corresponding rates in 2008 and 2010. There was an increase in rates of being bullied in 2008 but then a decrease by 2010. The initial increase might have been due to greater awareness and reporting of bullying, with rates then falling as the intervention takes effect. In fact this pattern – of an increase before a decrease in victimization rates – is a common finding when interventions are first introduced, and shows the importance of getting a sequence of data over some time period rather than a simple 'before-and-after' assessment.

REACTIVE STRATEGIES

A reactive strategy is a response to a bullying incident when it happens. Schools have a range of possible strategies to use here. In the

UK, the Department for Education (DfE) guidance states that "There is no single solution to bullying which will suit all schools", but that nevertheless "Schools should apply disciplinary measures to pupils who bully in order to show clearly that their behaviour is wrong". What schools actually do in England was ascertained by a national surrey in 2010 of anti-bullying practices.[3] Almost all did use some sanctions, but these were sometimes just limited to serious talks. Many used restorative approaches, and a minority used some non-punitive method.

Direct sanctions

The term *disciplinary measures* implies some kind of direct sanction for the perpetrator of bullying. However these can vary considerably in severity. At the lower end is a serious talk and verbal reprimand from the class teacher or head teacher; many schools will use this as a first step. Moving up the scale, the school may call in parents or carers for a meeting with the head teacher. Or, the bullying pupil may be temporarily removed from the class, or banned from the playground for a period, or have some privileges and rewards withdrawn. Further disciplinary measures include detentions, or punishment such as litter-picking or school clean-ups. Serious or recurring episodes may lead to temporary exclusion. A final resort would be permanent exclusion from the school.

The sanctions that schools use typically vary according to the type of bullying, the severity of the bullying and whether it is a first offence or a repeated pattern of behaviour. The survey of schools in England found that, in primary schools, sanctions were the preferred strategy for physical bullying; whereas in secondary schools, sanctions were used more widely for bullying through damaging belongings, race-related bullying, homophobic bullying and cyberbullying.

There is a clear rationale for sanctions (partly expressed by the aforementioned DfE guidance). It is a public consequence for the bullying pupil(s) that demonstrates that bullying is unacceptable, in line with the school anti-bullying policy; it shows that school rules and policies are to be taken seriously. It can promote pupil understanding of the limits of acceptable behaviour, for the bullying pupil(s) but also for others. The bullying pupil(s) should be confronted with the harm that they have caused and learn from it. There is also a deterrent function for disciplinary measures; the punishment should deter any repetition by the bullying pupil(s), and also deter other pupils from doing any similar behaviours.

What kind of sanctions work best? There has been little study of this, but one investigation in the US[4] used what is called *time hazard modelling of incidents*. The researchers gathered data from 122 schools across seven states, focussing on 1,221 pupils who had received a disciplinary referral for bullying. They looked at what method of discipline was used, and whether the pupil got a second referral in same school year. Comparing the different disciplinary methods, a number had no significant effect, including time in office (e.g. with principal), detention and in-school or out-of-school suspension. However two methods had significant positive impact, reducing the changes of a subsequent referral; these were loss of privileges, and parent-teacher conference (parents come into school to discuss the situation with teaching staff). Interestingly, one method, parent contact (just informing them what had happened), had a significant negative impact. Not all parents may share the anti-bullying attitudes of the school, especially some parents of bullying children, and this finding indicates that thorough involvement with parents may be necessary to harness their ability to influence bullying behaviours in a positive direction.

School tribunals/bully courts

Disciplinary methods are carried out by school staff; in England, all school staff can use milder forms of sanction but only the head and deputy headteachers can temporarily and permanently exclude students. However one method does bring in pupils themselves to have a say in what sanction(s) should be used. These are school tribunals, sometimes called bully courts. These were initially tried out in Canada. They had some notoriety in England in the 1990s; at the time they were advocated by Kidscape, a national charity concerned with children's safety from bullying and abuse, which claimed high levels of success for this method.

The school tribunal or bully court makes use of an elected body of pupils. This group will meet after an alleged incident has occurred. A teacher chairs the court, but the intention is to leave decisions to the pupils as much as possible. The court interviews those involved: perpetrator(s), victim(s) and also any witnesses. It then decides what punishment (if any) is appropriate.

The positive rationale behind school tribunals is that it allows pupils a say in behaviour that affects them, and may harness peer group attitudes against bullying in an effective way. However it is not popular with teachers, who feel that it gives too much power to pupils in matters that may be quite serious. Sometimes pupils give quite heavy sanctions that teachers may feel inappropriate. As a result the method is seldom used.

Non-Punitive Methods

Disciplinary measures have some clear rationale, but there can also be objections to them. It can be argued that a disciplinary measure is intended to cause harm to someone (the bullying perpetrators), who find it difficult to defend themselves (the pupils are less power-ful than the teacher or the school); and if this is repeated, the school might be modelling the kind of bullying behaviour that they are supposedly trying to stop! Repeated negative sanctions might actu-ally provoke resentment in a pupil who may already be somewhat disaffected with the school. Put another way, negative sanctions may temporarily prevent bullying but may not change the attitudes and long-term behaviour patterns of the pupil being punished.

A number of teachers and anti-bullying practitioners, reasoning along these lines, prefer less punitive approaches, at least for the less severe incidents of bullying. Two well-known methods, with system-atic procedures to follow, are the Pikas Method of Shared Concern and the Support Group Method.

The Pikas Method or method of shared concern

This method was developed by a Swedish psychologist, Anatol Pikas, in the late 1980s, and has been used by schools in, for example, Sweden, England and Scotland and Australia over subsequent decades. The method has evolved a bit over this period, but the essentials are relatively unchanged.

Pikas argued that the bullying perpetrators usually function as a group (even if one is the ringleader), mutually reinforcing each other in their actions. Applying direct sanctions to this group, he argued, might actually be counter-productive. Instead he advocated a non-punitive approach which uses a combination of individual and group meetings to break through the group dynamic of bullying. The method uses a combination of a simple script with specific non-verbal cues. The method is best carried out by an external counsellor, or else by a teacher in the school not directly involved with the pupils, and training is needed to ensure a thorough grasp of the technique. It has five consecutive phases:

1 *Individual talks with suspected bullies*: the adult starts by arranging for the suspected ringleader bully to be invited for an individual chat in a room which is quiet and where there will be no interruptions. The chat is not confrontational, but starts with the comment that there is a problem, since others have witnessed that the bullied pupil is unhappy and has experienced bullying. The adult follows a semi-structured script, usually leading to mutual agreement that the bullied pupil is unhappy, and then the adult asking "what can you do to improve the situation?". Common outcomes are that the pupil says he or she will leave the bullied pupil alone or tell others to stop, or become more friendly towards him or her.

Noteworthy here is that the suspected bullies are not directly accused of anything. They are simply asked what they know about it and what they can do to help. Of course, they may admit to taking part in the bullying, but this is not required.

After concluding this session, the adult mentions that he or she will see some other pupils now (mentioning their names) and that he or she will come back next week to see how things are going. She or he indeed goes on to interview each other pupil suspected of bullying, individually, in a similar way.

2 *Individual talk with the victim*: a supportive chat with the bullied pupil follows. Here Pikas feels it important to distinguish between the 'passive' victim and the 'provocative' victim (see Chapter 2). For passive victims it is a matter of reassurance, and the message that the bullying pupils have promised to change. For provocative victims it is a matter of helping them understand that they contribute to their own problems, and that their own behaviour, as well as that of the bullying pupils, should change.

3 *Preparatory group meeting*: the adult meets with the suspected bullies, as a group now, to see if they have kept to their agreements and can say something positive when the victim joins them.

4 *Summit meeting*: a meeting of all pupils involved is held to reach public agreement for reasonable behaviour on all sides and to determine long-term strategies for maintaining co-operative behaviour.

5 *Follow-up of the results*: a check, some while later, that the joint agreement made has been followed.

This approach is expected to sensitize bullying children to the harm they are doing to the victim, encourage positive behaviours to the victim and also encourage provocative victims to change their behaviour in positive ways.

An evaluation in Australian schools[5] found the method 'highly successful' in improving the situation for bullied students and 'generally helpful' in improving the attitudes and behaviour of bullying pupils, with practitioners endorsing its use for bullying. The surveys of both Australian and English schools found that only a minority used the Pikas Method. It does require a trained adult to use the method properly, preferably someone with counselling-based experience, and this is not always available. Although often successful, sometimes the bullying pupils may switch their attention from the initial victim to another child outside of the group. In the case of very persistent bullying, further interventions may be required.

Support Group Method (seven steps approach)

The Support Group Method (SGM) was developed in England by Barbara Maines and George Robinson in the 1990s. It adopts a problem-solving approach, run by an adult facilitator. A support group is formed for the bullied pupil, and this group is given some responsibility for solving the problem and for reporting back on progress. Like the Pikas Method, it aims to arouse a sense of empathic concern for the pupil who has been bullied, and to elicit responsible action to help resolve the problem. However it differs in the steps involved. There are seven steps in the SGM:

1 *Talk with the bullied pupil:* this can take place at home or in school. The bullied pupil is encouraged to talk in general terms about their experiences. He or she is reassured that the bullies will not get into trouble. The aim of the interview is to find out what happened and who has been involved, with a focus on the feelings of the bullied pupil, rather than on the details of the episode. It is helpful for the pupil to describe his/her feelings in writing, a poem or a drawing.

2 *Convene a group meeting:* from the pupils named in the interview, the adult convenes a group at school of around six to eight pupils, including those involved in the bullying episode (bully, assistants), bystanders and friends of the victim. The bullied pupil is not included. The group is told that the bullied pupil has a problem and that they have been chosen to help him or her. The group is reassured that they will not get into trouble.

3 *Communicate to the group how the bullied pupil feels:* the facilitator describes how the victimized pupil feels about their experience, having got prior permission from him or her. This is often done using

the writing or drawing that he or she produced in the earlier interview (step 1). There is no interrogation of individuals in the group, and no one is blamed for what has happened.

4 *Share responsibility*: some members of the group may be uncomfortable or upset at what they have heard, or anxious that they are going to get into trouble. The facilitator re-emphasizes that the purpose of the group meeting is to solve the problem, not to apportion blame. The atmosphere is non-judgmental, so that the group can address the problem-solving task openly. The group are encouraged to take joint responsibility for the situation.

5 *Elicit helpful suggestions*: suggestions about how to help the bullied pupil are obtained from the group. Groups vary widely in the extent to which they can produce suggestions, but it is usual for some group members to produce ideas spontaneously. If ideas are not forthcoming, it may be useful to go back over the incidents that caused upset. The actual suggestions are less important than the development of a group commitment to action.

6 *Hand over responsibility to the group*: the facilitator ends the meeting by thanking the group for its participation in helping the bullied pupil and complimenting it on the quality of the ideas. The group is given responsibility for implementing some actions based on the suggestions made. An agreement is made to meet each group member individually a week later to review progress.

7 *Individual meetings with participants*: the facilitator interviews each member of the group, and the bullied pupil, individually, to establish how successful the intervention has been. Each pupil reports back on his or her contribution to the resolution of the problem.

The SGM aims to develop emotional awareness, peer support and social skills and empathy of pupils involved. It does not aim for retribution or punishment. In fact, the SGM was originally called the No Blame approach. This was not inappropriate, as at stage 2, convening the group meeting, it was recommended to start proceedings by saying that "we are not blaming anyone for what has happened".

However the phrase 'No Blame' was inappropriate in the sense that it aroused opposition from a number of sources, including politicians and charities such as Kidscape, that felt it was irresponsible to let bullying children off from any kind of consequences for their actions. Renaming the approach as the Support Group Method did not change the approach itself, but it did make it more palatable in certain quarters.

The survey of English schools found that a minority of schools used the SGM, mostly for relational and verbal bullying, reporting that it encouraged pupils to take responsibility for their actions through empathy with the bullied pupil. Schools were divided over the effectiveness of the method, with some liking its non-confrontational, non-punitive approach, whilst others saw it as an avoidance of assigning blame or responsibility. It was also found that the SGM was adapted considerably in use, so that the 'seven steps' were not always followed as outlined. One problem mentioned was the extent to which parents should be consulted or informed of the procedure. A common view was that the SGM was worth trying for less serious cases, but that sanctions needed to be available as a backup.

Restorative approaches

While direct punishment may be counter-productive sometimes, non-punitive approaches are open to the accusation that despite having an anti-bullying policy or ethos, bullies can behave the way they do without incurring any clear negative consequences. Restorative approaches provide something of an intermediate way between punitive and non-punitive methods. They do aim to hold the perpetrators responsible for their actions, and to acknowledge the harm that they have caused, but they do not necessarily invoke any punishment or negative sanction beyond this. A main focus is to have a meeting or conference of those involved, aiming at 'restoring' good relationships, rather than on 'retribution'. The emphasis is less on "you have broken the school rules and this must stop", and more on "(the victim) has felt hurt by what you have done; what can you do to help make things better and restore good relationships?"

Some of the ideas were originally derived from the concept of the New Zealand Maori 'family conference'. It was developed by Transformative Justice Australia, and then extended to Canada, the US and Europe. Within the UK, restorative approaches were originally taken forward in the area of youth justice and criminal behaviour, and later taken on board in the educational sector.

Three main principles of restorative approaches are as follows:

1 *Responsibility*: the perpetrator learns to accept responsibility for the harm or offence caused through their actions;
2 *Reparation*: the victim is involved, and reparative activities are devised to help the perpetrator(s) alleviate some of the harm and distress they have caused;
3 *Resolution*: successfully ending a dispute so that the pupils are free to interact without threat of further conflict.

This kind of approach does need a skilled facilitator, and it is also helpful if pupils are used to discussing their feelings and relationship issues. A good background for this is prior use of *problem solving circles* or *circle time*. Here, under teacher supervision, pupils in a class arrange their chairs in a circle and discuss a problem which needs resolving. All pupils are given the opportunity to speak, but only one is able to talk at any given time. Pupils are largely positive to circle time in terms of learning about and expressing feelings and solving problems. This kind of routine activity will help make restorative approaches smoother and more effective.

The actual restorative approach used will depend on the nature and severity of the bullying incident. It can range from simple pupil-based discussions through to a full restorative conference. A basic technique is to make the perpetrator aware of the victim's feelings through the use of a series of diagnostic questions, and to encourage the perpetrator to acknowledge the impact of what he or she has done and to make amends. In a *short* or '*mini*' *conference*, an informal meeting is held between the pupils involved, led by a trained member of staff, in which incidents and harm caused are examined, and the offender(s) are asked to discuss possible means of reparation. In a *full restorative* conference, a formal, structured meeting takes place involving pupils, along with their parents/carers, friends and school representatives, who are brought together to discuss and resolve an incident. The staff member leading this kind of conference needs to be highly trained. He or she should hold individual interviews with the participants, prior to the full conference, to ensure that this is appropriate and that everyone is prepared for it.

Use of restorative approaches in schools has grown rapidly in recent years and are being increasingly used for all types of anti-social behaviour, including bullying. The survey of English schools found that a majority claimed to be using restorative approaches to some extent. However only about half of these had undergone formal training in the method; if teachers have not had sufficient training or experience in good practice, this can be problematic, especially for a full conference which needs to be handled carefully.

Some evaluations have reported successful outcomes of using restorative approaches, but some also raise important concerns. It is thought necessary that schools commit fully to a restorative ethos, adopting a whole school approach that is supported by senior management and backed up by adequate training in restorative techniques for staff. If this is not done, tensions can arise with any prevailing, sanction-based practices. The restorative approach is in contrast to the retributive approach of sanctions, but, in practice, if a pupil refuses 'to restore' or does not abide by the decisions reached, schools may still need to resort to sanctions.

EVIDENCE ABOUT THE EFFECTIVENESS OF DIFFERENT APPROACHES

There has been, and remains, controversy over the most effective ways to deal with perpetrators of bullying when an incident occurs. Should they experience discipline in the form of some negative sanction? This is often advocated, and indeed if someone infringes an agreed whole-school policy on bullying, it may seem logical that some disciplinary punishment follows. On the other hand, some psychologists coming from a more counselling-based approach argue that such negative sanctions may be counter-productive, making bullying per-petrators even more resentful of the school and of the anti-bullying values being promoted. There are not many good sources of evidence that compare the effectiveness of these different approaches. But there are a few, and three are mentioned here, from Finland, England and Australia.

A study in Finland[6] made use of the national KiVa anti-bullying intervention program, described later in Chapter 7. All the KiVa schools implemented an anti-bullying program, but so far as reac-tive strategies were concerned, they were randomly assigned to either a Confronting or Non-confronting approach. The Confronting approach was disciplinary, with some negative sanction for the pupil who had bullied. The Non-confronting approach followed the phi-losophy of the Pikas or SGM methods, focussing on the hurt of the victim and what could be done to help him or her.

Altogether 65 schools (33 Confronting, 32 Non-confronting) pro-duced detailed data on the outcomes of the two approaches, based on victim reports. Analyzing 339 cases, the researchers found that the bullying had stopped in 78% of the cases. Initially it appeared that the Confronting approach was more successful (83%) than the Non-confronting approach (73%), but this difference disappeared when characteristics of the incidents, especially the duration of the bullying, were taken account of. The Confronting approach was some-what more successful in secondary schools and for short-term vic-timization, while Non-confronting was somewhat more successful in primary schools, and for longer-term victimization. According to Christina Salmivalli,[7] who has directed the KiVa program, "Data col-lected during seven years of nationwide dissemination of the KiVa program provides no evidence of one approach (confronting vs. non-confronting) being superior to the other. What seems to be impor-tant, instead of the approach itself, is a systematic follow-up".

The survey in England involved data from 31 schools and 285 incident reports. These reports were gathered from both teachers and pupils (victims). Four approaches were compared for success, as shown in Table 6.1; serious talks were very commonly used as a first

Table 6.1 Percentage of bullying incidents where the bullying stopped completely, by sector and type of bullying; from 285 incident report forms in 31 schools in England

| | Total | Sector | | Type of bullying | | | |
		Primary	Secondary	Physical	Verbal	Relational	Cyber
Serious talk	65	58	71	62	61	66	73
Direct sanctions	62	58	65	60	61	60	75
Restorative approaches	73	68	77	67	73	76	73
Support Group	76	80	71	60	68	100	60
Overall	67	61	71	62	65	69	70

step, and so were separated out from other, somewhat more severe, direct sanctions. Not enough schools used the Pikas Method for this to be analyzed. The findings are divided by sector (primary or secondary schools) and by the main type of bullying involved (physical, verbal, relational or cyber).

The overall success rate was around 67%, but this did vary by method, sector and type of bullying. Direct sanctions were somewhat less effective than SGM, especially for relational bullying. This difference in success rates was less for secondary than primary schools. Also, for cyberbullying (but not other types of bullying), direct sanctions were the most effective. This study also found a high rate of success for restorative approaches, especially in secondary schools and with physical and verbal bullying.

The third source of evidence comes from a survey of 25 schools in Australia.[8] This relied on teacher ratings of effectiveness, and compared six strategies – the four surveyed earlier, plus Mediation (two pupils in conflict meet with a mediator) and Strengthening the victim (developing social and assertive skills, which is usually more of a proactive strategy). On a 5-point scale (where 3 = no effect, 4 = positive effect, 5 = very positive effect), the mean ratings were highest for Restorative practice (4.14) followed by Strengthening the victim (4.04), Mediation (4.04), Support Group Method (3.92), Pikas Method of Shared Concern (3.83) and lastly Direct sanctions (3.77).

These three sources of evidence do vary somewhat in which strategy comes out the best. The Finnish and English data do agree however that, relatively, sanctions may be more effective at the secondary school level, and non-punitive approaches at the primary school level. It is possible that non-punitive approaches, which aim to increase empathy for the victim, are easier at younger ages; this is discussed further in Chapter 7. Another general conclusion may be that all these strategies have a reasonable level of effectiveness, and what may be most important is consistency of approach, a clear school philosophy and effective follow-up of incidents when they happen.

7

THE WIDER CONTEXT

This final chapter will first point out how our increased knowledge of school bullying has helped design effective programs of intervention. Some, notably the Olweus Bullying Prevention Program in Norway, the KiVa program in Finland and the ViSC program in Austria, have been very successful in their home countries and are being tried out elsewhere. Some factors affecting the degree of success of interventions will be considered. The role of politicians and of charities in supporting anti-bullying work will be mentioned. The chapter will end by considering again the distinction between bullying and aggression, discussing how bullying can happen in other contexts than schools and pointing to helpful websites as well as sources for further reading.

INTERVENTION PROGRAMS

In Chapters 5 and 6 we looked at a number of proactive, peer support and reactive strategies that schools can employ. They have a choice, and in many countries this *à la carte* approach is common when starting anti-bullying work. For example in England, the government pack *Don't Suffer in Silence*, active from 1994 to 2002, presented just such a range of strategies for schools to select from.

An alternative might be called a *set menu* approach. A planned, hopefully optimum, combination of strategies is developed to form an intervention program. This program can then be disseminated on a wide scale, through training and publications, and evaluated for success. A number of such programs now exist. The *à la carte* vs. *set menu* distinction will be returned to later.

THE OLWEUS BULLYING PREVENTION PROGRAM (OBPP)

As mentioned in Chapter 1, the systematic history of anti-bullying interventions, at least in western countries, started in Norway. A nationwide anti-bullying campaign was initiated in Norway in autumn 1983. This was in response to the suicides of three boys in late 1982 due in large part to school bullying. The early research by Olweus and others provided evidence that the problem of school bullying was not confined to a few isolated cases, but was rather frequent and endemic. This evidence was very important, as otherwise it is tempting for schools, education authorities and politicians to say that what happened (for example, suicides) were exceptional cases and that widespread action is not necessary.

Such a negligent response did not happen in Norway. Instead, an initial program of intervention was designed on a national scale. This was fairly basic: the main elements were as follows:

- A pupil-based survey to assess the nature and extent of bullying problems in each school.
- A booklet for school personnel, giving information on bullying and suggestions for dealing with it
- A 20-minute video showing episodes of bullying as a basis for class discussion.
- A folder with information and advice for parents.

This was disseminated nationally, but Olweus carried out an evaluation of the impact of the intervention in Norway's second city, Bergen. In doing so, he worked with schools to expand the basic elements, and this quickly evolved into the first version of the Olweus Bullying Prevention Program (OBPP). The OBPP has a number of components at different levels:

- Individual-level components (serious talks and intervention plans for involved students).
- classroom-level components (class meetings and meetings with parents).
- School-level components (Bullying Prevention Coordinating Committee, introducing school rules against bullying, doing a questionnaire survey).
- Community-level components (supportive partnerships with community members).

The overall philosophy of the OBPP is for adults to act as responsible and authoritative role models: to be both warm and supportive to students, but to set firm limits to unacceptable behaviour such as bullying (this is very similar to the authoritative school climate discussed in Chapter 5). There should be negative consequences when rules are broken (such as if bullying is perpetrated); but these should be non-physical and not overtly hostile.

Olweus carried out an evaluation of this augmented program in 42 primary and junior high schools, with some 2,500 students, in what is called the First Bergen Project, from 1983 to 1985. Normally, an evaluation of an intervention would compare *experimental* (having the intervention) and *control* (not having any intervention) schools. But as this study was during a national intervention campaign, it was not very feasible to compare what happened in the experimental schools with others, as they too would be having some intervention.

Of course it would be possible to compare the same children before and after (perhaps just before the intervention started, and a year later). But this would be problematic. Victim rates decrease with age naturally (as discussed in Chapter 2). So Olweus designed a procedure called *time-lagged contrasts between age-equivalent groups*, or alternatively called an *extended selection cohorts* design. Consider a class of children in (say) grade 4. After a year of intervention, they are in grade 5. They are a year older, so any decrease in victim rates might be a natural age effect, unconnected with the intervention. But suppose we compare these new grade 5 children with those who had been in grade 5 a year ago, just before the intervention started? We have now controlled for age, so any difference is likely to be due to the intervention. Of course different children are now being compared, and this might be a problem in a small study in one or a few schools; a few unusual (e.g. highly victimized) pupils might distort the findings. But with a study in 42 schools, this is unlikely to be a systematic problem.

Using this approach, Olweus carried out before and after self-report assessments from pupils, using his Olweus Bully/Victim Questionnaire (Chapter 2). On this basis he estimated that in schools using the OBPP, victim rates fell by around 50% over a 2-year period. This reduction was similar for both boys and girls. Comparing the 42 schools, he also found that greater teacher involvement in the program, and better implementation, correlated substantially with how large these reductions in levels of victimization were.

A reduction of a problem such as school bullying by 50% is very encouraging. True, the issue has not gone away. But it is difficult to make significant impact on problems so deeply rooted in aspects of human nature, as bullying arguably is. This finding, as it was disseminated amongst researchers and educationists towards the end of the 1980s, inspired the next generation of researchers. My own work in this area was prompted by a visit to Norway in 1988, where I first learnt of this research. In the next few years, further interventions were carried out and evaluated in England, Canada and the Flanders area of Belgium, in part based on the OBPP model, but also used with other or different components.

Olweus continued his intervention work, long after the first national campaign had ceased. He used a more conventional intervention/control school design in a New Bergen project, from 1997 to 1998. Surveys were carried out in 14 intervention and 16 comparison schools. After six months, victim and bully rates had decreased in intervention schools, with little change or an increase in comparison schools. A subsequent Oslo project, from 1999 to 2000, in 37 schools, again found substantial effects.

A new Norwegian National Initiative against Bullying was launched in Norway in autumn 2001. All schools were expected to develop a plan for anti-bullying work, but could decide their own strategy or adopt the OBPP or another program designed by Erling Roland, called Zero. This national initiative provided an opportunity to examine the effects of the OBPP with very large samples of students and schools, and again substantial reductions were found.

The positive impact of the OBPP has thus been well replicated in Norway. It has been used in other countries too, including Germany, Iceland, Lithuania, the Netherlands and the US, with some but usually much less consistent success. This may be because of changes in how the program is implemented, or may reflect cultural differences in what kinds and combinations of components are most effective.[1]

THE KIVA PROGRAM

The KiVa anti-bullying program was developed in Finland between 2006 and 2009 by Christina Salmivalli and colleagues. KiVa is short for *Kiusaamista Vastaan*, or against bullying; and the acronym *kiva* also means nice or good in Finnish. The program is partly based on the participant role approach to bullying (Chapter 2). It sees the peer context as an essential aspect of effective anti-bullying work, with peer defenders having an important role. KiVa includes *universal interventions* (for everyone, e.g. via the classroom); and *targeted interventions* (for those involved as bullies or victims). There is also a parents' guide.

The universal interventions involve student lessons (in primary school) and theme days (in secondary school), with discussions, video films and exercises on topics such as the dynamics and consequences of bullying, and the actions students can take in order to support victimized peers. A notable feature is the use of a virtual learning environment (VLU) – an anti-bullying computer game for primary students, and an internet forum *KiVa Street* for secondary students. In the VLU pupils face a number of challenging situations in the playground, lunchroom and school corridors; decide how to respond to these situations and receive feedback on the choices they have made. Each level has three modules: I *Know* (pupils are presented with facts about bullying), I *Can* (pupils practice the skills they have learnt) and I *do* (encouraging pupils to transfer the knowledge and skills acquired in the virtual environment, into real life interactions with peers).

The targeted interventions are based around teams of three adults in the school. Incidents of bullying are referred to them; they discuss the situation with the pupils involved and provide support for the victimized student. (The actual procedure with the bullying perpetrator may vary, as described in Chapter 6). Meanwhile the classroom teacher meets with selected high-status classmates of the victimized children, asking them to provide support (as we saw in Chapter 2, high-status peers can have more impact as defenders).

In 2007–2008 a *randomized control trial* (RCT) evaluation was carried out. In an RCT, schools are randomly assigned to experimental (intervention) and control (no intervention – in practice, perhaps delayed a year) conditions; this is generally regarded as the strongest evaluation design. To assess victim and bully rates, both self-report and peer report data was gathered (Chapter 2). By the end of the year, the KiVa intervention schools showed significantly greater reductions than the control schools on most measures, of the order of 20–30%. Encouragingly, these reductions were found for all kinds of bullying, including cyberbullying. However, effects were less, or not significant, for the oldest age group, grades 7–9 (about 14–16 years in Finland).[2]

These findings were generally encouraging, and following this, KiVa was rolled out across the country, with a national launch in autumn 2009. By 2011 some 90% of all comprehensive schools in the country were using it. A further evaluation during 2009–2010 used the extended selection cohorts design (as an RCT was now not feasible). Generally, the KiVa program reduced bully and victim rates, though somewhat less than in the RCT trials, perhaps because the RCT trial attracted particularly motivated schools.

Kiva is now being tried out in several countries, including the Netherlands, Estonia, Greece, Italy, Sweden, Wales and the US. As an example, successful use of the program was reported in a study in Italy.[3] Here 13 schools were randomly assigned (by tossing a coin!) to intervention (7) or control (6) conditions, with a total of 97 classrooms and 2,184 pupils participating, from grade 4 (primary school) and grade 6 (middle school). The KiVa program was used with only minor modification of materials for the Italian context, over one school year. Measures included self-reports of being a victim or perpetrator, as well as of attitudes to bullies and victims, and empathy expressed toward victims. The main findings for victim and perpetrator (bully) rates, and empathy, were that in primary schools:

- The intervention brought about a decrease in victim rates, and in bully rates; these did not decrease in the control schools.
- Empathy for victims increased substantially more in the intervention schools.

and in middle schools:

- The intervention again brought about a decrease in victim rates, and in bully rates, although to a lesser extent than in the primary schools; but there were increases in the control schools.
- Empathy for victims increased more in the intervention schools, although this finding was not statistically significant.

Overall these are encouraging results, even if (as usual) the effects are stronger for younger children.

THE ViSC PROGRAM

In Austria, the ViSC school program is one part of a national strategy against violence in schools (Spiel & Strohmeier, 2011).[4] Activities are geared to increasing social competence in the school as a whole, in classrooms and on the individual level. The class project consists of 13 units, covering alternative ways to perceive, interpret and deal with critical situations using vignette stories, discussions and role-plays. An evaluation using intervention and control classes found greater reductions in victim rates in the intervention classes, post-test and at follow-up 4 months later; and a greater reduction in rates of bullying others in the intervention classes, at follow-up only. Another analysis,[5] with a randomized control trial, found effectiveness in reducing cyberbullying and cyber-victimization, sustainable at the 6 months follow-up. The program has also been used in Cyprus, with more success at grade 7 than at grade 8.

STEPS TO RESPECT

A number of anti-bullying programs have been developed in the US. One well-known program is Steps to Respect, designed for children in grades 3 to 6 (about ages 8 to 11). Besides developing school-wide policies and procedures and emphasizing staff training, it has a social-emotional skills curriculum designed to help students develop empathy, emotion regulation, conflict resolution skills, positive and supportive peer relationships and to change attitudes towards bullying. Evaluations comparing intervention and control schools have reported some positive findings,[6] including less acceptance of bullying and greater reported bystander responsibility in intervention schools, and greater improvements in school climate; but no significant changes in pupil-reported levels of victimization or bullying perpetration.

FRIENDLY SCHOOLS INITIATIVE

The Friendly Schools initiative is an intervention program for primary schools in Australia. This again is a whole school approach, with a focus on curriculum work to build social skills such as conflict resolution, empathy, prosocial skills and peer discouragement of bullying. It also includes family involvement, for example through newsletters sent to parents. A comparison of intervention and control schools[7] found some positive outcomes, including fewer reported observations of bullying behaviours and self-reports of being a victim, although not in self-reports of bullying perpetration.

INTERVENTIONS FOR CYBERBULLYING

Cyberbullying has its own features (Chapter 2), but we do know that often the same pupils are involved in traditional and cyberbullying and victimization. Therefore interventions to reduce bullying generally, even if focussed mainly on traditional bullying, should be relevant for cyberbullying as well. For example, curriculum work to include empathic awareness, conflict resolution, prosocial behaviour, might be expected to have an impact on cyberbullying. In fact the KiVa intervention in Finland and the ViSC intervention in Austria found that reductions were just as substantial for cyberbullying as for traditional bullying. In Australia the Friendly schools program has been expanded to Cyber Friendly Schools. This operates at individual, family, peer, online and community levels, and has had some positive outcomes.

More specific interventions relevant to cyberbullying are likely to be helpful. This type of bullying should be mentioned explicitly in school policies and guidelines for internet behaviour, and e-safety skills (Chapter 5) are important. There are many sources of website advice for children and young people, parents and schools. In addition a number of more specific programs have been developed.[8] For example, *Media Heroes*, developed in Germany, includes elements on cyberbullying (such as consequences, legal background), as well as more general social skills and empathy training. In the Netherlands, a web-based intervention called *Online Pestkoppenstoppen* has been tried out. This consists of web-based advice sessions covering rational problem-solving, coping strategies and internet safety. It is a tailored intervention, meaning that participants fill in questionnaires on their personality and favoured coping strategies, with the advice sessions being adjusted correspondingly.

META-ANALYSES OF THE SUCCESS OF ANTI-BULLYING INTERVENTIONS

By now quite a large number of anti-bullying programs have been evaluated, and a number of meta-analyses have been carried out, to assess how effective they are in general. Most evaluations have been in Europe and North America, but there has also been work in eastern countries such as Japan, South Korea, mainland China and Hong Kong. One very thorough analysis[9] analyzed 44 school-based intervention programs and found that, on average, they reduced bullying and victimization by around 20%. Further meta-analyses have been reported.[10] These also find some degree of success achieved by anti-bullying interventions in schools, although much of the work has been in primary schools.

SET MENU OR À LA CARTE APPROACHES?

Well-established anti-bullying programs, such as OBPP, KiVa, ViSC, Steps to Respect, Friendly Schools and several others, have a well-defined set of components to use, which operate at various levels (e.g. whole school, class, individual). Some actions are preventative, or proactive, laying a foundation of respect in interpersonal relationships. Some are more reactive, being ways to respond when bullying happens. Both proactive and reactive strategies are likely to be needed in any comprehensive approach.

One theoretical perspective could be taken as strong support for a set menu approach – and one that should be very extensive.[11] This invokes a theory from social psychology called the Theory of Planned Behavior. Essentially, this suggests that a successful intervention would require changes in *perceptions* (e.g. of what bullying is), *attitudes* (about bullying behaviour and towards victims, reporting bullying and intervening), *subjective norms* (how do others think or expect I should behave?) and *efficacy beliefs* (feeling confident that actions such as reporting or defending will be successful and not result in negative consequences) in order to ultimately change actual *behaviours*. Taking ideas from organizational science, it is also argued that it is necessary to target these, not only with pupils, but with teachers and other staff in the school or relevant to the school. All these would be necessary if changes in the *school culture* (assumptions, values and beliefs) are to match up with changes in the *school climate* (actual behavioural changes in, for example, bully and victim rates).

The *set menu* approach can be contrasted with an *à la carte* approach, in which schools choose from a range of components, selecting those that they feel most appropriate for their situation. This might have the advantage that schools feel more ownership of their anti-bullying actions, and may choose components most suitable to their needs and philosophy, rather than being asked to fit into a pre-existing framework.

Programs such as OBPP and KiVa have had replicated success, suggesting that they do make a successful package to use. But programs are not always followed as closely as might be hoped or intended. For example in KiVa, it was found that out of 10 lessons planned, teachers actually delivered an average of 8.7 in the RCT trial, falling to 7.8 during the first year of the national rollout, and to 7.2 in the second year. Schools can vary greatly in implementation, impacting on success in the reductions of victim and bully rates.

In fact, one study carried out with 39 Swedish schools[12] showed that the difference between set menu and à la carte can be over-stated. This is because schools and teachers tend to adapt programs that are presented to them. This study started by aiming to compare the success of eight anti-bullying programs (such as the OBPP). What they actually found was that all the schools supposedly using one particular program, were in reality using components from more than one program; and even eight schools selected as non-intervention 'controls' were doing so as well! Thus the focus of their evaluation changed from comparing programs to comparing program components (such as those discussed in Chapters 5 and 6).

SUCCESS OF INTERVENTIONS AT DIFFERENT AGES

As noted previously several times, interventions seem to be relatively more successful at younger ages: at primary more than at secondary level. An in-depth analysis of this[13] found 19 studies where the impact on different age levels could be compared directly. It showed that, up to grade 7, programs were generally effective; but that in grade 8 and beyond they had little if any effect. There are a few individual successes, but it appears to be a greater challenge to reduce bullying in mid-adolescent school pupils.

There are reasons why this might be so. Adolescents (more than younger children) are very concerned with status in the peer group, and we saw (Chapter 3) how bullying can be used to gain power and status in the peer group. Attitudes to victims tend to be most negative around mid-adolescence. Adolescents are also more resistant to exhortations from teachers than are younger children. Organizational factors in large secondary or high schools may also impact on the effectiveness of interventions.

EVOLUTIONARY PERSPECTIVES AND MEANINGFUL ROLES

A particular perspective on age differences in bullying, and the success of interventions, as well as recent developments in understanding brain changes and risk-taking behaviour in adolescence have come from evolutionary psychology.[14] The argument advanced here is that bullying is a universal phenomenon, found in hunter-gatherer societies and throughout different historical epochs; that it is prevalent (not of course that all children are bullies, but that it is found at appreciable levels rather than being a very occasional phenomenon); that it has a genetic basis (as shown by twin studies, Chapter 2) and that bullying can have advantages for the pupil who bullies. The advantages include gaining dominance and social status (and hence access to resources); having better individual growth, strength and health and individual reproductive success (using measures such as attractiveness to and dating or sexual opportunities with the opposite sex). More succinctly, these are reputation, resources and reproduction. These are particularly important in adolescence, as young people start to jockey for position and status in the adult world. A successful bully may ultimately have greater reproductive success (more children), and pass on genes that are predisposed to bullying to the next generation.

This argument is supported by recent work on the adolescent brain,[15] which shows how brain remodelling in adolescence involves a set of regions called the social brain. These are particularly activated during perspective-taking tasks, impulse control, processing emotional states of others, concern for self vs. ideas of trust and sharing, peer influence, peer evaluation and fear of rejection. These brain areas change more rapidly than those mediating cognitive regulation and control. In other words, there is a temporary imbalance, for a few years in mid-adolescence, where sensitivity to social and emotional rewards outpaces cognitive control. This can lead to greater self-focus in adolescence, greater reward-seeking and increased risk-taking (for example to impress others and gain status).

Such evolutionary theorists argue that bullying is a *facultative adaptation*. This means that the propensity to bully may be latent in most or all of us, but will be expressed to a greater or lesser extent depending on the circumstances. A decision to bully is based (largely unconsciously) on a cost/benefit analysis of the consequences. If so, this naturally could have consequences for anti-bullying interventions. A challenge for working with bullies would be to change behaviour in those for whom the bullying is providing benefits and low costs. Indeed, an analysis of the KiVa program, discussed earlier, found that it reduced bullying rates in bullies who were less popular or of average popularity in the peer group, but it did not do so with bullies who were popular.

Not everyone accepts the arguments of these evolutionary theorists, and the benefits to bullying behaviour will clearly depend a lot on context, and may be over-stated. But if there were some truth in the arguments, what can be done about this? One suggestion is the *meaningful roles* approach. Proponents of this believe that, especially in secondary schools, the status benefits from bullying are such that alternative, prosocial, status-enhancing activities need to be provided for such popular bullies. In the meaningful roles approach, all pupils, but especially those inclined to bully, are given prosocial activities with some responsibility that helps them have respect in the peer group, such as helping run activities, organizing sporting competitions, acting as peer tutors. The feasibility and success of such an approach in reducing bullying behaviour still needs to be ascertained. However this approach does suggest that we need to be aware of the likely costs and benefits are for the bullying child. Simple adult sanctions that 'bullying is wrong' might be counter-productive. Effective action needs to acknowledge the social competence and perceived popularity of many bullies, and the status gains they seek and may get from bullying.

COST/EFFECTIVENESS OF INTERVENTIONS

A factor in implementing interventions on a wide scale will be cost. We have seen how successful programs can reduce victimization. Given the consequences associated with victimization (Chapter 4), such programs can be expected to reduce mental health costs and have benefits for educational achievement and later productivity. But, such benefits need to be balanced against costs – of materials and of teacher time, for example. It may not be too hard to assess the costs of an intervention, but assessing the benefits is more difficult. Nevertheless, from a political point of view it is important to show that benefits can be expected to outweigh costs.

A few publications have started to examine the cost-effectiveness of anti-bullying programs. One[16] examined the cost-effectiveness of the OBPP in terms of what tax increases people would be prepared to accept in order to implement such a program in their local schools. On this basis, they concluded it was a cost-effective intervention. Another approach might be to estimate costs of the likely damage done to victims (for example costs of extra mental health provision and reduced earnings).

SUSTAINABILITY AND SOCIETAL CONTEXT

Beyond the actual programs, or program components, it is important to consider the wider societal context in which interventions take place. An intervention or campaign, even a national one such as that in Norway, may have immediate positive effects, but it is of limited value if it produces quite good results for a short period, only for things to slip back once the project is finished. To produce long-term sustainable change, it is helpful to have national organizations that maintain awareness of the issue, provide resources and keep pressure up on politicians and governments to support anti-bullying work. Examples are PrevNet, in Canada, which is focused on knowledge mobilization, conferences and publications; the Anti-Bullying Alliance (www.anti-bullyingalliance.org.uk) in England, which brings together over 50 national organizations and has supported the development of a portfolio of resources, and anti-bullying weeks held annually; and the National Safe Schools Framework (NSSF) in Australia which encourages the sharing of information, resources and successful practices, and encourages schools to adopt whole school programs.

Looking beyond schools, factors such as violence in the media, and levels of violence in communities, have been shown to be related to levels of bullying, at least at a correlational level. Violence in the media, and in video and computer games, has often been cited as an influence on aggression, although the extent of this remains debated. A common conclusion is that there can be harmful effects of such violence, but that for most children, it is not a major factor in understanding violent behaviour. Nevertheless some studies have established links between violent media exposure, and involvement in bullying or cyberbullying, and it is likely that these can affect children already predisposed to act this way.

Some issues are more political and very long term, such as levels of income inequality (see Chapter 3). These, and country-level differences (as for example in the EU Kids Online model) are at the outer levels of the ecological model (Figure 3.1).

OTHER CONTEXTS FOR BULLYING

In this book we have considered bullying amongst children and young people, primarily in schools but also via the internet. The origins of the term seem to lie here, most research has been done in this area and some definitions explicitly limit bullying to school-aged children (Chapter 1).

The research on childhood and school bullying is vigorous. It has gathered a lot of knowledge over some 30 years. Furthermore, this knowledge has been put to good use in designing school-based intervention programs. These programs have had some success. They are far from 100% effective, but they do make a difference, and we are learning more about the difficulties and challenges, and what is likely to make interventions more effective.

Nevertheless this body of work might be considered as narrow. This is in two quite different ways, although both hinge on the definition of bullying. One concerns the differentiation of bullying from aggression. The other concerns the school and children context.

Bullying and aggression: in Chapter 1 we discussed how bullying differs from aggression more generally, in terms of the criteria of repetition, and imbalance of power. We also saw how these criteria can be challenged, especially in the cyber domain. A number of researchers prefer to talk about cyber aggression, rather than cyberbullying. A more general case was put by David Finkelhor and colleagues in an article titled "Let's prevent peer victimization, not just bullying".[17] Here, they argued not only that the two criteria had problems (for example, imbalance of power can be difficult to measure), but also that individual acts of aggression (such as a severe physical attack, or a school shooting) can be very harmful. They suggested that more focus on harmful aggression generally was called for.

Of course, harmful acts of aggression deserve study and intervention, but this need not detract from the importance of studying bullying specifically. Several studies[18] do indicate that the criteria of repetition and power imbalance can not only be measured, but do predict the depth of harm that aggressive acts cause. In other words, bullying is one particularly nasty and harmful kind of aggression – and one that is quite prevalent.

Bullying in different contexts: if we take the hallmark of bullying to be a systematic abuse of power, then clearly it has much broader application than the school and childhood contexts. However other words, such as abuse, or harassment, may be more commonly used (in English), in contexts such as the family or the workplace.

Unless we use a narrow definition of bullying, then it applies to parent-child abuse in the family. It could apply to abuse in children's homes and institutions. It can apply to abuse in sports contexts, for example by a coach. It can apply to harassment in the workplace (often referred to as workplace bullying) and similarly to prisons and the armed forces. It can apply to elder abuse in old people's homes. In fact, all these are contexts where it is difficult for someone to leave, such that repeated attacks by a more powerful person may continue.[19]

Ultimately, we are looking at an issue of human dignity and human rights. Long ago, Dan Olweus wrote that "it is a fundamental democratic right for a child to feel safe in school and to be spared the oppression and repeated, intentional humiliation implied in bullying".[20] Not only is this a worthy aspiration, but it can be applied to the lifespan (not just to children) and to many contexts (not just school). Indeed at the time of writing, abuse of children in sports settings, and in children's homes; and abuse of younger women by powerful men in politics, and the media, are in newspaper headlines on almost a daily basis. A more comprehensive approach to bullying, abuse, harassment – in terms of terminology, in terms of raising awareness, in terms of delineating what is and is not acceptable and in terms of coping strategies and interventions – may be forthcoming in the future. For now, the studies of school bullying, while still a work in progress, can be considered as an exemplar of how researchers and practitioners have worked together to gather knowledge, and also apply it in real-life settings; I believe to the benefit of many children now and in years to come.

SOME USEFUL WEBSITES

www.anti-bullyingalliance.org.uk/
> Comprehensive website on all kinds of bullying, part of National Children's Bureau and organizes anti-bullying week.

www.ditchthelabel.org/
> Anti-bullying charity, dedicated to promoting equality and provides support to young people who have been negatively affected by bullying and prejudice.

www.bullying.co.uk/cyberbullying/
> Bullying UK, part of Family Lives, is a leading charity providing advice and support to anyone affected by bullying.

www.childnet.com/
> Childnet advises on internet safety and has a range of leaflets for children and parents in different languages, including Hindi, Punjabi and Maltese.

https://cyberbullying.org/
> Charity dedicated to cyberbullying, has plenty of useful advice on combating cyberbullying, including how to take screenshots of online bullying for evidence.

www.anti-bullyingalliance.org.uk/tools-information/all-about-bullying/cyberbullying-0
> Website dedicated to cyberbullying (and bullying), has plenty of useful information about cyberbullying and how to seek help.

www.thinkuknow.co.uk/

> Thinkuknow (education program from the National Crime Agency) aims to empower children and young people aged 5–17 to identify the risks they may face online and know where they can go for support.

www.getsafeonline.org/

> Awareness resource that helps protect yourself and your family from fraud, abuse and other issues encountered online.

www.kidscape.org.uk/cyberbullying/

> Its focus is on children's safety, with an emphasis on the prevention of harm by equipping children with techniques and mindsets that help them stay safe.

www.internetmatters.org/issues/cyberbullying/

> Provides guidance about the many issues children can experience when using the internet.

www.saferinternet.org.uk/

> Online safety tips, advice and resources to help children and young people stay safe online.

INTERNATIONAL WEBSITES

http://www.antibullying.eu/

> The European Antibullying Network (EAN) brings together practitioners and researchers from many European countries.

https://ibpaworld.org/

> The International Bullying Prevention Association is based in the USA but brings together practitioners and researchers internationally.

https://cehs.unl.edu/BRNET/

> Also based in the USA, the Bullying Research Network promotes international collaboration among researchers.

APPS

Bully Button: Bully Button allows children to record incidents and send them to adults with a single click of a button.

ReThink: ReThink™ provides an important opportunity for adolescents to change their minds and not post hurtful messages online. With a moment to pause, review and reconsider their decisions online, adolescents learn to make better choices on and off of the internet (for more information www.rethinkwords.com/)

GUIDANCE FOR SCHOOLS

www.gov.uk/government/publications/preventing-and-tackling-bullying

> Guidance for schools on preventing and responding to bullying – guidance documents from the UK Government. Includes a document on cyberbullying.

FURTHER READING

BULLYING GENERALLY

K. Rigby (2010). *Bullying Interventions in Schools* (ACER)

P.K. Smith (2014). *Understanding School Bullying* (Sage)

T. Migliaccio & J. Raskauskas (2015). *Bullying as a Social Experience* (Ashgate)

CYBERBULLYING

S. Bauman (2011). *Cyberbullying —What Counselors Need to Know* (ACA)

J. Patchin & S. Hinduja (2012). *Cyberbullying Prevention and Response* (Routledge)

R. Kowalski, S. Limber, & P. Agatston (2012). *Cyberbullying* (Blackwell/Wiley)

NOTES

CHAPTER 1

1 Hayes, R. & Herbert, C. (2011). *Rising above bullying: From despair to recovery*. London and Philadelphia: Jessica Kingsley.

2 Webster, D. & Webster, V. (2012). *So many everests*. Oxford: Lion Hudson.

3 Mooney, S. & Smith, P.K. (1995). Bullying and the child who stammers. *British Journal of Special Education*, 22, 24–27.

4 Olweus, D. (1993). *Bullying at school: What we know and what we can do*. Oxford: Blackwell.

5 Lee, S-H., Smith, P.K. & Monks, C. (2012). Meaning and usage of a term for bullying-like phenomena in South Korea: A lifespan perspective. *Journal of Language and Social Psychology*, 31, 342–349.

6 Ditch the label. (2017). *The annual bullying survey 2017*. DitchtheLabel.org

CHAPTER 2

1 Slee, P., Skrzypiec, G., Sandhu, D. & Campbell, M. (2018). PhotoStory: A legitimate research tool in cross-cultural research. In P.K. Smith, S. Sundaram, B. Spears, C. Blaya, M. Schafer & D. Sandhu (eds.), *Bullying, cyberbullying and pupil well-being in schools: Comparing European, Australian and Indian perspectives*. Cambridge: Cambridge University Press.

2 Olweus Bully/Victim Questionnaire. University of Bergen, Norway. olweus@uni.no See also https://www.pdastats.com/PublicFiles/Olweus_Sample_Standard_School_Report.pdf

3 Tellus4 Evaluation. (2010). http://webarchive.nationalarchives.gov.uk/20120 503103309/www.education.gov.uk/publications/eOrderingDownload/ DFE-RR002.pdf

4 *The Annual Bullying Survey 2017.* Ditchthelabel.org

5 Student reports of bullying: Results from the 2015 school crime supplement to the national crime victimization survey. https://nces.ed.gov/pubsearch/ pubsinfo.asp?pubid=2017015

6 See Smith, P.K., Robinson, S. & Marchi, B. (2016). Cross-national data on victims of bullying: What is really being measured? *International Journal of Development Science*, 10, 9–19.

7 Juvonen, J., Nishina, A. & Graham, S. (2001). Self-views versus peer perceptions of victim status among early adolescents. In J. Juvonen & S. Graham (eds.), *Peer harassment at school: The plight of the vulnerable and victimised.* New York: Guildford, pp. 105–124.

8 Huitsing, G. & Veenstra, R. (2012). Bullying in classrooms: Participant roles from a social network perspective. *Aggressive Behavior*, 38, 494–509.

CHAPTER 3

1 Bronfenbrenner, U. (1979). *The ecology of human development.* Cambridge: Harvard University Press.

2 Smith, P.K. (2014). *Understanding school bullying: Its nature and prevention strategies.* London: Sage.

3 Salmivalli, C., Lagerspetz, K., Björkqvist, K., Österman, K. & Kaukiainen, A. (1996). Bullying as a group process: Participant roles and their relations to social status within the group. *Aggressive Behavior*, 22, 1–15.

4 Hong, J.S. & Espelage, D.L. (2012). A review of research on bullying and peer victimization in school: An ecological system analysis. *Aggression and Violent Behavior*, 17, 311–322.

5 Harter, S. (1985). *Manual for the self-perception profile for children.* Denver, CO: University of Denver.

6 Smith, P.K. (2017). Bullying and theory of mind: A review. *Current Psychiatry Reviews*, 13, 90–95.

7 Peeters, M., Cillessen, A.H.N. & Scholte, R.H.J. (2010). Clueless or powerful? Identifying subtypes of bullies in adolescence. *Journal of Youth and Adolescence*, 39, 1041–1052.

8 Ball, H.A., Arsenault, L., Taylor, A., Maughan, B., Caspi, A. & Moffitt, T.E. (2008). Genetic and environmental influences on victims, bullies and bully-victims in childhood. *Journal of Child Psychiatry and Psychiatry*, 49, 104–112.

9 Kärnä, A., Voeten, M., Poskiparta, E. & Salmivalli, C. (2010). Vulnerable children in varying classroom contexts: Bystanders' behaviors moderate the effects of risk factors on victimization. *Merrill-Palmer Quarterly*, 56, 261–282.

10 Bibou-Nakou, I., Tsiantis, J., Assimopoulos, H. & Chatzilambou, P. (2012). Bullying/victimization from a family perspective: A qualitative study of secondary school student' views. *European Journal of Psychology of Education*, 28, 53–71.

11 Anti-Bullying Alliance. *Sexual bullying: Developing effective anti-bullying practice.* www. anti-bullyingalliance.org.uk

12 Stonewall. (2017). *School report: The experiences of lesbian, gay, bi and trans young people in Britain's schools* in 2017. www.stonewall.org.uk/get-involved/education

13 Lereya, S.T., Samara, M. & Wolke, D. (2013). Parenting behavior and the risk of becoming a victim and a bully/victim: A meta-analysis study. *Child Abuse & Neglect*, 37, 1091–1108.

14 Cornell, D. & Huang, F. (2016). Authoritative school climate and high school student risk behavior: A cross-sectional multi-level analysis of student self-reports. *Journal of Youth and Adolescence*, 45, 2246–2259.

CHAPTER 4

1 Guldberg, H. (2010). *Sorry, but it can be GOOD for children to be bullied.* www. dailymail.co.uk/femail/article-1281630/DR-HELENE-GULDBERG-Sorry-GOOD-children-bullied.html

2 Smith, P.K., Talamelli, L., Cowie, H., Naylor, P. & Chauhan, P. (2004). Profiles of non-victims, escaped victims, continuing victims and new victims of school bullying. *British Journal of Educational Psychology*, 74, 565–581.

3 Frisén, A., Hasselblad, T. & Holmqvist, K. (2012). What actually makes bullying stop? Reports from former victims. *Journal of Adolescence*, 35, 981–990.

4 Kanetsuna, T., Smith, P.K. & Morita, Y. (2006). Coping with bullying at school: Children's recommended strategies and attitudes to school-based interventions in Japan and England. *Aggressive Behavior*, 32, 570–580.

5 Wright, M.F. (2016). Cybervictims' emotional responses, attributions, and coping strategies for cyber victimization: A qualitative approach. *Safer Communities*, 15, 160–169.

6 Veiga Simão, A.M., Costa Ferreira, P., Freire, I., Caetano, A.P., Martins, M.J. & Vieira, C. (2017). Adolescent cybervictimization – Who they turn to and their perceived school climate. *Journal of Adolescence*, 58, 12–23.

7 Machmutow, K., Perren, S., Sticca, F. & Alsaker, F.D. (2012). Peer victimisation and depressive symptoms: Can specific coping strategies buffer the

negative impact of cybervictimisation? *Emotional and Behavioural Difficulties*, 17, 403–420.

8 Wolke, D. & Lereya, T. (2015). Long-term effects of bullying. *Archives of Disease in Childhood*, 100, 879–885.

9 Arseneault, L. (2018). Annual research review: The persistent and pervasive impact of being bullied in childhood and adolescence: Implications for policy and practice. *Journal of Child Psychology and Psychiatry*, 59, 405–421.

10 Cyberbullying tragedy: New Jersey family to sue after 12-year-old daughter's suicide. https://www.nbcnews.com/news/us-news/new-jersey-family-sue-school-district-after-12-year-old-n788506

11 Ttofi, M.M., Farrington, D.P. & Lösel, F. (2011). Do the victims of school bullies tend to become depressed later in life? A systematic review and meta-analysis of longitudinal studies. *Journal of Aggression, Conflict and Peace Research*, 3, 63–73.

12 Farrington, D.P., Lösel, F., Ttofi, M.M. & Theodorakis, N. (2012). *School bullying, depression and offending behaviour later in life: An updated systematic review of longitudinal studies*. Stockholm: Swedish National Council for Crime Prevention.

13 Nansel, T.R., Craig, W., Overpeck, M.D., Saluja, G., Ruan, W.J. & The Health Behaviour in School-aged Children Bullying Analyses Working Group. (2004). Cross-national consistency in the relationship between bullying behaviors and psychosocial adjustment. *Archives of Pediatrics and Adolescent Medicine*, 158, 730–736.

14 Brown, S. & Taylor, K. (2008). Bullying, education and earnings: Evidence from the National child development study. *Economics of Education Review*, 27, 387–401.

15 Rivers, I., Poteat, V.P., Noret, N. & Ashurst, N. (2009). Observing bullying at school: The mental health implications of witness status. *School Psychology Quarterly*, 24, 211–223.

CHAPTER 5

1 Ennis, J. (2012). *Unbelievable - From My Childhood Dreams To Winning Olympic Gold*. London: Hodder & Stoughton.

2 Ttofi, M.M. & Farrington, D.P. (2011). Effectiveness of school-based programs to reduce bullying: A systematic and meta-analytic review. *Journal of Experimental Criminology*, 7, 27–56.

3 Cowie, H. & Smith, P.K. (2010). Peer support as a means of improving school safety and reducing bullying and violence. In B. Doll, W. Pfohl & J. Yoon (eds.), *Handbook of youth prevention science*. New York: Routledge, pp. 177–193.

4   Menesini, E., Nocentini, A. & Palladino, B.E. (2012). Empowering students against bullying: and cyberbullying: Evaluation of an Italian peer-led model. *International Journal of Conflict and Violence*, 6, 313–320.

5   Thompson, F. & Smith, P.K. (2013). Bullying in schools. In N. Purdy (ed.), *Pastoral care 11–16: A critical introduction*. London: Bloomsbury, pp. 64–95.

6   Purdy, N. & Smith, P.K. (2016). A content analysis of school anti-bullying policies in Northern Ireland. *Educational Psychology in Practice*, 32, 281–295.

7   Cornell, D., Shukla, K. & Konold, T. (2015). Peer victimization and authoritative school climate: A multilevel approach. *Journal of Educational Psychology*, 107, 1186.

CHAPTER 6

1   Department for Education. (2017). Preventing and tackling bullying: Advice for headteachers, staff and governing bodies. www.gov.uk/government/publications

2   Ramirez, M., Ten Eyck, P., Peek-Asa, C., Onwuachi-Willig, A. & Cavanaugh, J.E. (2016). Evaluation of Iowa's anti-bullying law. *Injury Epidemiology*, 3(1), 15.

3   Thompson, F. & Smith, P.K. (2011). *The use and effectiveness of anti-bullying strategies in schools*. DFE-RR098; and Thompson, F. & Smith, P.K. (2012). Anti-bullying strategies in schools – What is done and what works. *British Journal of Educational Psychology*, Monograph Series II, 9, 154–173.

4   Ayers, S.L., Wagaman, M.A., Geiger, J.M., Bermudez-Parsai, M. & Hedberg, E.C. (2012). Examining school-basded bullying interventions using multi-level discrete time hazard monitoring. *Prevention Science*, 13, 539–550.

5   Rigby, K. & Griffiths, C. (2010). *Applying the method of shared concern in Australian schools: An evaluative study*. Canberra: Department of Education, Employment and Workplace Relations (DEEWR).

6   Garandeau, C.F., Poskiparta, E. & Salmivalli, C. (2014). Tackling acute cases of school bullying in the KiVa anti-bullying program: A comparison of two approaches. *Journal of Abnormal Child Psychology*, 40, 289–300.

7   C. Salmivalli, personal communication, 01/11/2016.

8   Rigby, K. (2016). School perspectives on bullying and preventative strategies: An exploratory study. *Australian Journal of Education*, 61, 24–39.

CHAPTER 7

1   Olweus, D. & Limber, S. (2010). The Olweus bullying prevention program: Implementation and evaluation over two decades. In S. Jimerson, S. Swearer &

D. Espelage (eds.), *Handbook of bullying in schools: An international perspective*. New York: Routledge, pp. 377–401.

2 Salmivalli, C. & Poskiparta, E. (2012). KiVa antibullying program: Overview of evaluation studies based on a randomized controlled trial and national rollout in Finland. *International Journal of Conflict and Violence*, 6, 294–302.

3 Nocentini, A. & Menesini, E. (2016). KiVa anti-bullying program in Italy: Evidence of effectiveness in a randomised control trial. *Prevention Science*, 17, 1012–1023.

4 Spiel, C., & Strohmeier, D. (2011). National strategy for violence prevention in the Austrian public school system: Development and implementation. *International Journal of Behavioral Development*, 35, 412–418.

5 Gradinger, P., Yanagida, T., Strohmeier, D. & Spiel, C. (2016). Effectiveness and sustainability of the ViSC social competence program to prevent cyberbullying and cyber-victimization: Class and individual level moderators. *Aggressive Behavior*, 42, 181–193.

6 Brown, E.C., Low, S., Smith, B.H. & Haggerty, K.P. (2011). Outcomes from a school-randomized controlled trial of *Steps to Respect*: A bullying prevention Program. *School Psychology Review*, 40, 423–443.

7 Cross, D., Monks, H., Hall, M., Shaw, T., Pintabona, Y., Erceg, E. et al. (2011). Three year results of the friendly schools whole-of-school intervention on children's bullying behavior. *British Educational Research Journal*, 37, 105–129.

8 Campbell, M. & Bauman, S. (eds.) (2018). *Reducing cyberbullying in schools*. London: Elsevier.

9 Ttofi, M.M. & Farrington, D.P. (2011). Effectiveness of school-based programs to reduce bullying: A systematic and meta-analytic review. *Journal of Experimental Criminology*, 7, 27–56.

10 Smith, P.K. (2016). School-based interventions to address bullying. *Estonian Journal of Education*, 4, 142–164.

11 Hawley, P.H. & Williford, A. (2015). Articulating the theory of bullying intervention programs: Views from social psychology, social work, and organizational science. *Journal of Applied Developmental Psychology*, 37, 3–15.

12 Flygare, E., Frånberg, G-M., Gill, P., Johansson, B., Lindberg, O., Osbeck, C. & Söderström, Å. (2011). *Evaluation of anti-bullying methods*. Report 353. Stockholm: National Agency for Education. www.skolverket.se

13 Yeager, D.S., Fong, C.J., Lee, H.Y. & Espelage, D.L. (2015). Declines in efficacy of anti-bullying programs among older adolescents: Theory and a three-level meta-analysis. *Journal of Applied Developmental Psychology*, 37, 36–51.

14 Ellis, B.J., Volk, A.A., Gonzalez, J-M. & Embry, D.D. (2016). The meaningful roles intervention: An evolutionary approach to reducing bullying and increasing prosocial behavior. *Journal of Research on Adolescence*, 22, 622–637.

15 Blakemore, S-J. & Mills, K.L. (2014). Is adolescence a sensitive period for sociocultural processing? *Annual Review of Psychology*, 65, 187–207.

16 Beckman, L. & Svensson, M. (2015). The cost-effectiveness of the Olweus bullying prevention program: Results from a modeling study. *Journal of Adolescence*, 45, 127–139.

17 Finkelhor, D., Turner, H.A. & Hamby, S. (2012). Let's prevent peer victimization, not just bullying. *Child Abuse & Neglect*, 36, 271–274.

18 Ybarra, M.L., Espelage, D.L. & Mitchell, K.J. (2014). Differentiating youth who are bullied from other victims of peer-aggression: The importance of differential power and repetition. *Journal of Adolescent Health*, 55, 293–300.

19 Monks, C. & Coyne, I. (eds.). (2011). *Bullying in different contexts*. Cambridge: Cambridge University Press.

20 Olweus, D. (1993). *Bullying at School: What We Know and What We Can Do*. Oxford: Blackwell, p. 48.